The Edge Data Center

The Edge Data Center

Building the Connected Future

Hugh Taylor

BUSINESS EXPERT PRESS

Leader in applied, concise business books

The Edge Data Center: Building the Connected Future

Copyright © Business Expert Press, LLC, 2023.

Cover design by nskvsky

Interior design by Exeter Premedia Services Private Ltd., Chennai, India

First published in 2023 by
Business Expert Press, LLC
222 East 46th Street, New York, NY 10017
www.businessexpertpress.com

ISBN-13: 978-1-63742-500-8 (paperback)
ISBN-13: 978-1-63742-501-5 (e-book)

Business Expert Press Collaborative Intelligence Collection

First edition: 2023

10 9 8 7 6 5 4 3 2 1

For Noam, Ezra, and Gavriel

Description

5G and related digital revolutions will require tens of thousands of edge data centers. This book tells you how they work and how to get them built.

We are in the middle of the edge computing revolution. Responding to demand for lower latency, telcos and others are moving servers and storage closer to end users—away from the *core* to *the edge*. This requires the deployment of many thousands of tiny edge data centers.

The edge is a big, growing business. Driven by 5G, connected vehicles, and industrial automation, the *edge economy* is projected to reach U.S.$4.1 trillion by 2030, with investment in edge data centers set to exceed U.S.$140 billion by 2028.

What exactly is an edge data center? This book explains what they are and how they work. It's early in the edge computing life cycle, so there's time to get prepared for what's coming.

If you work in an industry that's transforming through mobility, or any field that will leverage the edge for competitive advantage, this book will help you understand how the edge data center advances your strategic agenda.

Keywords

edge data center; edge computing; digital real estate; 5G; connected vehicles; data centers; enterprise technology

Contents

Foreword

Having spent 30 years in the IT infrastructure field, I want to consider myself immune to hype. That may be so much wishful thinking, because I've definitely proven to be susceptible to hype about edge computing. I'm even guilty of hyping the paradigm myself. However, like all hypers, I believe my own story.

Edge computing is experiencing the sort of jagged, unpredictable growth that typifies new technologies with a maddeningly unclear mix of use cases. Yet, I think even the calmest in my cohort would agree that edge computing is going to be big, perhaps extremely big. How big will the sector be? When will this growth occur? What will be the drivers of growth? These matters are far from settled or obvious.

That said, I will make a prediction or two. I suspect the growth in edge computing will come sooner than we expect. As the CEO of Edgevana, a business that helps Web3 companies deploy at the edge, I see the business trends that are pushing IT out of core hyperscale data centers. From this vantage point, I think we will be looking back, five or so years from now, and wondering how we could not have planned for more deployment— for more effective and efficient deployment, too.

I believe the world is short at least a billion square feet of data center space. Much of it will be at the edge. I know that sounds a bit loony, but I've been around long enough to see stranger forecasts come true. The technological and market pressures are easy to see. Smart device proliferation is accelerating. Cellular antenna density is increasing, a factor that will only get more significant as new generations of wireless connectivity come online. Edge use cases like blockchain infrastructure are expanding. Where else will all of this go except to new edge sites?

The reason it's difficult to predict the specifics is that the path from here to there is not well marked. We have many eggs but not enough chickens, so to speak. A lot of stakeholders seem to want someone else to make the first, big move, to shoulder the massive upfront investment. I suspect it won't be that simple a process. It will be a messy series of stages that will look preordained in retrospect.

This is the context for Hugh Taylor's book. What he's done is to provide a detailed look at the edge data center, the fundamental physical building block of the edge computing industry. The value in the material comes from his laying out, methodically, the major elements of the edge data center, the variations on its design and deployment, as well as the factors that affect its implementation. It thus promises to be a valuable companion for any analysis of the emerging edge computing category.

—Mark Thiele

CEO

Edgevana

Acknowledgments

I could not have written this book without the support and input of many people. I would like to thank, first of all, my wife, Rachel, for her unending support and encouragement—as well as her strength in listening to me speak endlessly about technology matters. Scott Isenberg of Business Expert Press and his colleague, Nigel Wyatt, made this book possible. I also want to acknowledge the contributions of Marc Feldman, Tony Grayson, Chris Hanks, Millie Lapidario, Lisa Latham, Al Madden, Aditya Mishra, Christopher Prewitt, Daniel Robbins, Michael Siteman, Mark Thiele, Denis Vilfort, and Ron Vokoun, without whom this book would not exist. Thank you all for your help and expert insights.

Introduction

Revolutions in information technology (IT) seem clear and inevitable when viewed from the comfort of the present day. For example, according to technology industry lore, the personal computer revolution started in 1981, when IBM introduced the first PC. The social media revolution took off in 2006, when Facebook started to accept members from everywhere, not just college campuses. The smartphone revolution began in 2007, with Steve Jobs debuting the iPhone, and so forth.

Except, none of these revolutions actually happened in the ways we think they did. IBM decided to build a personal computer after watching upstarts like Coleco and Radio Shack spend years turning toy computers into viable business machines. Facebook was not the first social network. By the time it ascended to its dominant position, networks like Friendster and MySpace had popularized the category and imploded. The iPhone emerged as the winner in the smartphone category a good decade after the Palm Pilot started to carve out the digital assistant category.

IT revolutions occur when an innovator builds on the work of others and solidifies a clear market leadership position with a product or service that breaks through the noise and truly changes the way people and businesses use technology. However, the revolution has typically started long before the innovator makes his or her mark on the industry. During this period, the trends and technology developments marking the way to the breakthrough are often muddled and difficult to parse.

The edge computing category is now in this early, prerevolutionary state. We are hearing a lot about it now, though it's not entirely clear what's happening. Vendors and industry analysts are hyping the idea of *the edge*. Industry analysts like Chetan Sharma predict the arrival of a U.S.$4.1 trillion *edge economy*.[1] The edge computing market is projected

---

[1] C. Sharma. 2019. *Edge Internet Economy: The Multi-Trillion Dollar Ecosystem Opportunity.*

to reach U.S.$87 billion by 2026.[2] The reality, though, is that a working, consensus-based definition of *the edge* remains elusive.

What is clear, however, is that edge computing requires placing computers closer to end users than is currently possible with large *hyperscale* data centers. Success—and the anticipated edge computing revolution—will involve the deployment of many small-scale *micro* edge data centers. Already available in a range of sizes and shapes, these petite structures will house the computers needed to process information close to end users' devices.

However the edge computing revolution unfolds, it will hinge on the development and installation of thousands of edge data centers. For this reason, an understanding of the edge data center is essential for grasping the potential of edge computing. That's the purpose of this book.

Edge Computing, in Brief

Edge computing refers to running a computer server in close physical proximity to software clients, which are typically mobile devices of some kind. The presence of a client/server software architecture is one of many details that tend to get glossed over in explanations of the edge. Edge computing places the server closer to the client so that it can respond more quickly to calls from the client.

The delay between a client's request for computing from the server and its receipt of the server's response is known as latency. For many use cases, latency is not an issue. The server responds in a fraction of a second, and the end user doesn't mind. However, a growing number of use cases require extremely low latencies, some as short as one millisecond, or one one-thousandth of a second. Ultra-low latency at the edge is emerging as a *must have* characteristic for autonomous vehicles, 5G services, gaming, and metaverses, to name just a few examples.

Latency increases with distance between client and server. This may not make sense, as the signals travel at the speed of light. The problem is the behavior of computer networks. The equipment and various *hops*

---

[2] Reportlinker. November 16, 2021. *The Edge Computing Market Size Is Expected to Grow From USD 36.5 Billion in 2021 to USD 87.3 Billion by 2026.*

between points on the network, slow down messages. In a business network, messages also queue up to get through to their destinations, adding more latency.

Edge computing cuts down latency by placing servers near the client. It stands in contrast to the standard client/server setup, wherein the client connects with a server hosted at a *core* data center. For example, for most mobile apps (the clients), the server is hosted at a hyperscale data center run by Amazon Web Services (AWS) or an equivalent provider. That data center might be hundreds of miles away—a location that contributes to high latency. The next chapter will probe these issues in greater depth.

Why I Wrote This Book

I felt that this book was necessary to help the many varied stakeholders in edge computing become familiar with the issues affecting the growth and evolution of the category. Some of these stakeholders may not even realize they have a role to play in edge computing. Automotive industry managers, for example, who would not consider themselves computer people, will likely have (or need) a voice in edge computing. This book will hopefully give them information and insights they need to participate in important dialogues that will affect their companies.

This book is intended for anyone involved in technology management, strategy, and business operations who will be affected by edge computing. On the technology side, edge computing is relevant to people who run networks and manage infrastructure. The edge data center is likely to become part of many enterprises' data center ecosystems. Software developers and enterprise architects also have a role to play in edge computing. This book may help them understand how the edge data center affects their work.

Edge computing is, or will soon become, a factor in industries ranging from telecommunications to finance, gaming, and metaverses to transportation and logistics. The edge is a key factor in the Internet of Things (IoT) and Industrial Internet of Things (IIoT). People who are tasked with making such businesses function successfully at the edge will need to understand the edge data center.

I am focusing on the edge data center, along with the software that powers it, because the edge is, at its heart, a physical and practical technology issue. While many speak of *the edge* as if it were an abstract concept like *the cloud*, edge computing is all about location, hardware, and software. It's a specific, detailed area of focus. The edge data center is key to understanding how it all works and what will make the edge a success.

What's Inside

This book covers the edge at a high level, but also in detail across several main focus areas. Chapter 1 goes into depth defining the edge and contrasting it with the core. It offers examples of edge computing use cases. Chapter 2 delves into drivers of the edge computing revolution. It looks at trends like 5G, smart devices, IoT, and smart cities, along with workforce mobility and digital transformation. The edge is an essential element of these trends.

Starting in Chapter 3, we start to define the edge data center. The chapter lays out the different form factors and modes of edge data center deployment. Chapter 4 asks and attempts to answer an important question, which is "Hasn't this problem already been solved?" Indeed, the idea of edge computing is not new, and several established companies, such as Akamai, have been doing edge computing for years. The short answer is *No*. However, modern requirements demand a much bigger and more widely distributed edge infrastructure.

Chapter 5 explores edge data center design and modes of deployment. Some edge data centers are miniature replicas of full-scale data centers, complete with electrical backup, security, and cooling. Others are more like robust equipment cabinets. A great deal of experimentation and innovation is now occurring in the category. Deployment varies from traditional colocation (CoLo) to *bare metal* hosting and the emerging *edge cloud* model.

Chapter 5 also explores the edge data center as a business model of its own. It is still early in the lifecycle for this concept, but entrepreneurs are developing ventures that offer the unique characteristics of edge data centers to customers. As these companies launch, some are leveraging existing business models, such as cell tower leasing, to enter the market.

Operational concerns occupy Chapters 6, 7, and 8. They deal with issues like connecting edge data centers to the Internet and solving the problem of electrical power. Edge data centers consume a significant amount of electricity, so their deployment assumes proximity to the power grid and sufficient electrical power to operation.

Operating an edge data center is looking like a challenging area of work. In terms of maintenance and support, they are the complete opposite of hyperscale facilities. With the edge, people who do maintenance and support must travel to remote locations. To avoid excessive costs in this regard, edge data center developers are exploring a variety of remote support technologies.

Security is the topic for Chapter 9. Edge data centers present a number of cybersecurity risks that are not present in traditional large-scale facilities. These are not insoluble problems, but the edge requires a new way of thinking about security. Physical security, for example, is a far more serious concern at the edge than it is at the core.

Edge data center site selection is the subject of Chapter 10. An edge data center comes with a variety of unique, potentially challenging parameters for its location. It needs to be placed where it can deliver low latency. It also has to be close to fiber and power—while also satisfying zoning and permitting issues. A new class of business is starting to offer specialized services to facilitate the siting of edge data centers.

Chapter 11 explores novel locations for edge data centers, such as space and military bases. Already, some innovators are launching edge data centers into space on specially built satellites. There, they can handle data processing in real time in orbit, which helps with many different space-based computing workloads.

Chapter 12 introduces the subject of multi-edge computing. This is my personal point of view on how the edge will develop. I believe that no single entity will control the entire edge. For the edge to work as a business, it will be necessary for edge computing instances owned by different corporations to interoperate with one another. This will require standards and technologies that facilitate such interoperation.

Understanding the Edge as a Moving Target

At this moment, it almost seems foolhardy to be writing a book about edge data centers. This is a rapidly evolving category, a moving target. This book may become obsolete within a few years, but the idea is to provide a way of thinking about the edge as it is now.

The future of edge computing will arrive in whatever form it will take. There's no way to know exactly what it will look like. However, current thinking will drive future actions. This has happened in countless technological revolutions. Entrepreneurs learn from the mistakes of earlier market entrants and build on their findings. This is how the iPhone, Facebook, and IBM PC came into existence. The edge will be no different. The point of this book is to help the reader understand where the edge data center is today, with an eye toward what it will become tomorrow.

Talking to Experts

Taking on the task of writing a book like this can be a blow to the ego. Despite your best efforts to convince yourself otherwise, you realize that you don't in fact, know everything. For this reason, I have sought experts who can fill in gaps in my knowledge. Throughout the book, you will find comments from subject matter experts in fields ranging from telecommunications to data center construction.

A Note on Technology Terms Used in the Book

This book is about technology, but I have tried to write it so that it can be understood by a generalist. I don't go into great technical depth. It's not a manual or a book of IT patterns. Rather, it's intended for people who have a stake in edge computing, but who may not have extensive knowledge of IT. My assumption, however, is that the reader will have a general understanding of how computers and IT systems work. Wherever I use a technological term or acronym, I will attempt to define it so readers will not struggle to comprehend the material.

With all of this in mind, if you're ready to learn about edge data centers, read on....

CHAPTER 1

The Edge

An Overview

Like so many concepts in information technology (IT), the edge has more than one definition. Add in the inevitable hype and distortion that occur when a technological paradigm starts to heat up, and things can get pretty confusing. This chapter is about defining the edge, what happens at the edge, and why it matters.

Defining the Edge

We all know what an edge is. It's the furthermost part of an object or physical space. An outer fence is at the edge of a property. Suburbs are at the edge of an urban area, and so forth. In IT, the edge refers to a location, either physical, logical or both, that's outside the core of the IT infrastructure.

Let's take a moment to flesh out the contrasts between the edge and the core. When IT professionals talk about *the core*, they are referring to two related but separate ideas. The first way to define the core is as the core of a network. Figure 1.1 depicts this relationship in a simplified reference architecture.

In a business setting, the network core represents the corporate network. A core, on-premises data center houses the corporation's computer servers and data storage. This data center might be situated at a colocation provider, too. Users who are on-premises access this computer and storage capability through the corporate network. Users who are off the premises, or at the network edge, may access the core data center through an Internet connection, a virtual private network (VPN), and so forth. In this view of the edge, the edge is a place on the network topology.

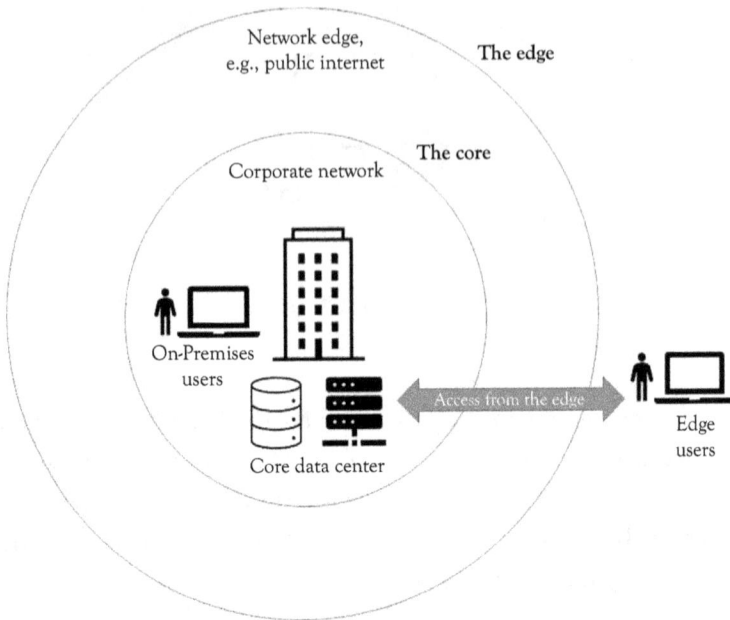

Figure 1.1 Relationship between the core and the edge

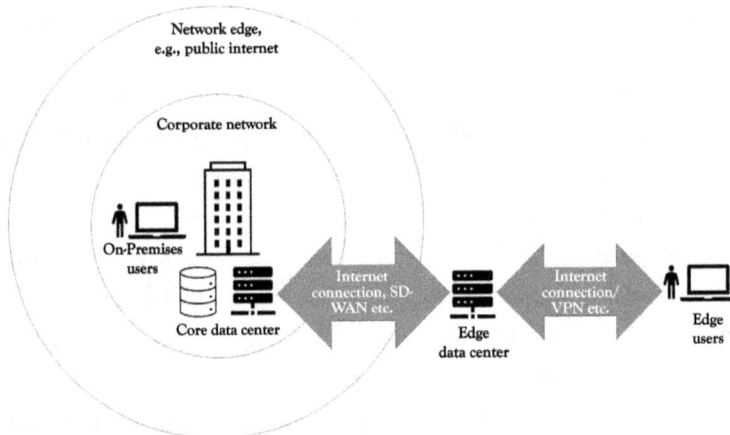

Figure 1.2 The edge data center puts computing at the edge of the network

The other way to define the edge is to make it about the location of computing and storage. Figure 1.2 adds an edge data center to the simple setup shown in Figure 1.1. Now, a user who is off the premises can access computing that is situated outside the core data center. He or she can connect with that edge data center over the Internet or through a VPN. The edge data center, in turn, typically connects with the core data center through some sort of wide area network (WAN). Today, this almost always means a software-defined WAN or SD-WAN, which uses encryption to establish a WAN connection over the public Internet or comparable private network.

In this view of the edge, the edge is a place where something is happening. This is the *computing* in *edge computing*. It's not just about network topology. This distinction may be useful when discussing what the edge is, and how it works.

The edge involves moving data and computer capacity closer to the end user. Why is this necessary? There are many reasons, but most of them have to do with cutting down the time it takes for data to move back and forth from the server to the end user. We will explore this idea in depth further along in this book.

These are highly simplified representations. In reality, a core data center could be on-premises corporate data center, an established colocation facility, or a hyperscale cloud data center such as one run by Amazon Web Services (AWS) or Microsoft Azure. The architectural principles remain the same, however.

Dialogues about the edge can get confusing when people from different industries come at the topic with differing perspectives on what constitutes the edge. While people from telecommunications, enterprise computing, and cloud computing companies might agree that the edge is a logical location at the furthest point from the core, the specifics of their viewpoints can be quite different.

For example, cloud/hyperscaler data center operators might see the edge as a city located outside a core geographic zone. A five-megawatt data center in Florida might be the *edge* of cloud core zone located in Northern Virginia, which has a 500-megawatt data center. That is not at all how an enterprise computing sees the edge. Their view might involve 8-kilowatt data centers in office buildings, situated a 100 yards away from a cell tower. The logical relationship is the same, but the distances and scales of data center footprints are quite different. Figure 1.3 depicts this architectural construct.

To confuse things a little more, there is a fourth way to define the edge, which is as the edge of a local network on corporate premises. In this point of view, the edge might be a Wi-Fi antenna located in the

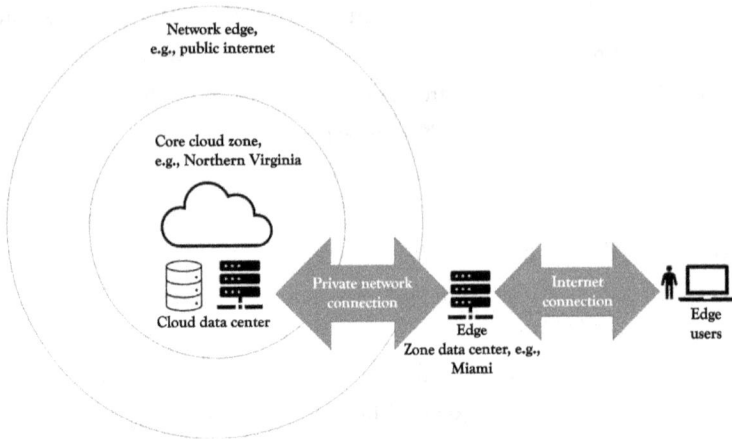

Figure 1.3 Cloud core zone versus edge zone

parking lot of a retail store. The parking lot is the *edge* of the store's local area network (LAN). Companies that specialize in networking hardware tend to use this definition of the edge.

It's a perfectly legitimate way to discuss the edge, but it is not relevant to discussions about edge data centers. So, I will ignore it from now on—but I wanted you to be aware of it because you may see advertising for *edge* equipment that has nothing to do with computer hardware and data centers.

The Edge Versus *The Edge*

Linguistic nuances matter in technology discussions. If you listen carefully to the way people talk about the edge, you may detect a difference between references to edge computing in general versus the edge as an industry paradigm. There's the generic edge, which refers to a network and infrastructure design. Then, there's *the edge*, which is an abstract but universal place comparable to *the cloud*. It's a worldwide collection of locations in cyberspace. This is the edge of industry analysts and big vendor visions. It also doesn't quite exist yet, but it's coming.

One important thing to note here is that some of these concepts are in operation via today's existing edge computing infrastructure. As I mentioned before, edge computing is not new. It's just accelerating as new technologies become available. For the last 20+ years, service providers like Akamai have been delivering data at the edge through content delivery networks (CDNs) based in telecom carrier hotels and facilities run by data center real estate investment trusts (REITs) like Equinix.

CDNs do not always deliver the ultra-low latency envisioned by the following use cases, and they don't currently operate at the scale required to service the burgeoning installed base of mobile devices. Also, at this point, CDNs do not offer a lot of depth in edge computing. Rather, they push content outward to devices. However, the CDN providers are in a great position to lead the way in edge computing, as they have an early presence in this growing market.

Selected Edge Computing Use Cases

As edge computing matures, a variety of industries will put the technology to work. At this point, a number of use cases are emerging, though over time, this list will probably start to look small. And, some of these predictions may fail to come true, as almost always happens with new technologies. What we think is about to happen is seldom what actually happens.

Games, Apps, and Entertainment

The faster a mobile device interacts with its user, the better that user's experience will be. This is particularly true for games and entertainment. Game players do not like delays in the experience, so they value low latencies. Catering to this audience, game makers and mobile entertainment providers are eyeing edge computing as a way to reduce latency.

This may seem like a trivial use case, but the reality is that mobile gaming and entertainment is a multi-billion-dollar industry. Mobile games now account for a full third of mobile app installs, 10 percent of mobile user time and nearly three-quarters of their consumer spend.[1] When this kind of money is involved, industry players will likely invest to keep customers happen and remain competitive.

---

[1] S. Perez. June 11, 2019. "Mobile Games Now Account for 33% of Installs, 10% of Time and 74% of Consumer Spend," *TechCrunch*.

Metaverses

Metaverses, those immersive virtual and augmented reality experiences, appear to be another significant use case for edge computing. While it is early in the lifecycle of metaverses, they represent the strategic direction of several major technology companies. Facebook's rebranding as Meta, with their stated goal of creating a metaverse, is representative of this trend. The multiuser, interactive nature of metaverses makes them a good candidate for ultra-low latency. Indeed, it would seem that a metaverse will not work well at all, from a user experience perspective, if avatar interactions are delayed by slow connections and sluggish computing on the server side.

Telecommunications

The telecommunications sector is now introducing edge computing services, some of which are related to the rollout of 5G wireless service. 5G promises faster data transmission and greater antenna density than 4G. The technology thus enables new services that can capitalize on these capabilities. However, in order for 5G services to work as advertised, computing must be present close to the mobile user. This may involve placing an edge data center close to the heart of the radio access network (RAN) infrastructure that makes 5G services work at cell tower sites. If data has to travel from a cell tower to a core data center and back to the end user, via the cell tower, the resulting latency will be too high to meet user expectations in most cases.

Multiaccess edge computing (MEC) is another example of the telecommunications industry's adoption of edge computing. MEC, previously referred to as *mobile edge computing*, extends cloud computing infrastructure to the edge of the telecom network. The idea is to shift the load of cloud computing away from core cloud data centers and move it closer to end users. In theory, an MEC site cuts down on congestion in mobile networks—reducing latency in the process and improving users' quality of experience (QoE).

Internet Services

Some edge computing use cases are an invisible part of other online experiences. For example, when an app or website gives you *autofill* suggestions on a form, those suggestions are often supplied via CDNs. With use cases like autofill, maps, and search suggestions, users expect lightning-fast interaction with the software. Even delays of a 100th of a second are noticeable and frustrating.

For this reason, Internet services like autofill are a compelling use case for the new generation of edge computing infrastructure. The customers for this edge infrastructure may be the big tech companies, for example, Apple, Google, and others. It's difficult to predict how their deployments would work, but it is likely they will need to build or rent capacity in numerous edge data centers.

Enterprise Computing

Enterprises, such as Fortune 500 companies, are the very definition of the core. They run large on-premises data centers, while also hosting compute and storage in the cloud and in colocation facilities. Enterprises are also good candidates for edge computing. Their uses for the technology include support for branch locations, industrial facilities, and mobile employees.

Transportation

The transportation sector is a frequent topic of discussion among advocates of edge computing. It is still something of a futuristic conversation, however. That doesn't mean it won't happen, but the use case remains somewhat hypothetical. Autonomous vehicles, for example, will need ultra-low latency computing nearly everywhere they go. They are envisioned as needing to interact with servers as they navigate roadways. Drones are expected to have a similar need. This will require true real-time responsiveness, a compelling use for edge computing. It is not clear what will happen, however. Some posit that autonomous vehicles will actually carry their computing onboard, with less need for interaction with external networks.

Internet of Things (IoT)

The Internet of things (IoT), like edge computing, is the subject of a fair amount of hype. Yet, it is happening. Industry, government, and scientific research endeavors are deploying billions of Internet-connected devices. These range from soil moisture sensors in agriculture to oil field temperature gauges and myriad other examples.

It's a big field already, though estimates vary when it comes to device counts. In 2017, the Ericsson Mobility Report put the census of IoT connective devices at 18 billion.[2] Statista claims there are currently 13 billion.[3] Whatever the number actually is, it's in the billions. The IoT is evidently a sizeable business, too. *Fortune Business Insights* pegged the IoT market at U.S.$384 billion in 2021, expanding at a compound annual growth rate (CAGR) of 26 percent.[4]

IoT use cases align well with edge computing, partly for reasons of latency, but also for convenience of not transporting data to core data centers. IoT devices can generate a great deal of data. In many cases, it is preferable to store and process that data closer to the devices themselves, rather than using up network capacity to move it the core. This requirement makes a good argument for edge computing and storage capacity.

Industrial Internet of Things (IIoT)

The industrial IoT (IIoT) is a subcategory of IoT. It encompasses specialized applications of IoT technology to industrial processes. These include maintenance sensors on industrial equipment and any number of Internet-connected devices that control the functioning of manufacturing machinery. An actuator on a valve in any oil refinery is one example. Robots are another. It's an enormous field, still at its early stages of life. Like the general IoT, IIoT favors the edge computing model for reasons of data management. Storing and processing IIoT data at the edge, perhaps even inside industrial facilities themselves, makes industrial operations go faster—enabling greater industrial productivity and profits in the process.

---

[2] P. Collela. 2017. "Ushering in a Better Connected Future." Ericsson.com.
[3] Statista—Number of Internet of Things (IoT) connected devices worldwide from 2019 to 2021, with forecasts from 2022 to 2030.
[4] Fortune Business Insights. 2021. "Internet of Things (IoT) Market Size."

Financial services

Companies that engage in financial trading have long been edge computing customers, even if they did not refer to the technology by that name. Stock and commodities trading, especially the trend toward high-frequency trading, demands low latency. Buying or selling a share of stock involves executing transactions on multiple, connected computer systems. It all happens quickly, but shaving even a fraction of a second off the execution of the trade can make a difference in the profitability of that trade.

As a result, financial firms strive to place computing capacity as close as possible to their trading floor operations. Office buildings on Wall Street, for example, all have data centers that support trading. The problem is that many of these data centers are maxed out in terms of physical space, electrical power, and network connectivity. Financial firms are looking for new ways to add trading computing capacity closer to their offices, which favors edge data center deployment.

Smart Cities

A growing number of municipalities are implementing *smart city* technologies with the goal of improving citizens' lives. These run the gamut from smart parking meters that can help people find places to park to intelligent traffic control systems that time traffic lights to minimize congestion. These solutions tend to rely on fast processing, which favors edge computing.

Call Centers

Call centers require a high concentration of bandwidth and computing capacity. In a call center, hundreds or even thousands of people are simultaneously using voice over IP (VoIP) phones and connecting with cloud-based software. Even in dense, urban areas, this workload may strain available network and computing. Edge data centers provide call center operators with rich telecom connectivity through fiber optic networks, coupled with localized computing capacity.

AI at the Edge

Artificial intelligence (AI) is a data- and computing-intensive workload. Although AI has many applications, they almost always involve processing large and diverse datasets to recognize patterns and make inferences from the data. In AI use cases where speed is of the essence, it may be preferable to store the dataset and run the AI software in an edge data center that is close to where the pattern recognition and insights are needed. The same is true for situations where it is impractical or excessively costly to transmit data over bandwidth to a core facility.

Space is an interesting example of this edge computing use case. Though in its infancy, space-based edge computing is starting to become a reality. Small data centers, for example, 4 kilowatts, are being launched into orbit on special satellites. There, they can ingest data, such as from sensors that track the movement of ships, and run AI analytics in real time. The satellite can develop and share insight on the data far more quickly than would be possible if the satellite had to transmit data to an earth station. In certain situations, such as in the military, that delay can defeat the entire purpose of the satellite's existence.

Military

The military is showing an interest in edge computing because warfare has becoming increasingly digital in nature. The command and control (C2) of weapons systems are almost entirely electronic now, as is the gathering of intelligence. In a war situation, the speed and accuracy of intelligence and C2 can be a life or death matter. So, the military is starting to deploy purpose-built edge data centers in so-called *forward* areas, near areas of military operation. For example, when a drone lands, it must disgorge a substantial amount of camera and radar data it has collected during its flight. This might be measured in multiple terabytes.

The faster the ground crew can offload this data for processing, the faster the drone can get back in the air—and the faster the intelligence command will have access to the data. An edge data center at the drone base is the solution. It obviates the need to transmit data from the drone to a core site, a process that will waste hours of valuable flight time in contrast to the speed of data transmission to a nearby edge site.

Web3

Web3, also known as Web 3.0, is a paradigm that describes the evolution of the World Wide Web. It is envisioned as the replacement for today's *Web 2.0* design, moving to a new decentralized model that utilizes technologies like blockchain and token-based economics to enable—in theory, at least—greater data security, privacy, and scalability. It is not clear that Web3 will live up to these promises, or even come to life at all. For some, Web3 is a flashy term that gives cover to localized cryptocurrency mining operations. In any event, Web3 is a use case for edge data centers. The small-scale and agile nature of edge data centers make them suitable for Web3 activities.

There is some controversy around Web3, however, as communities may not approve of small data centers that use up electricity for what many people view as an unproductive economic activity. It's an environmental issue, too, with community members potentially complaining about wasting energy on cryptocurrency creation and so forth.

Edge Computing Line of Business

Any of these use cases can be a business unto itself. Entrepreneurs are building businesses that offer AI at the edge, smart city edge solutions, and so forth. Others are piloting purpose-built computing hardware and edge data center solutions. Existing players like telecom companies are similarly launching commercial offerings based on edge computing. The Wavelength Zones alliance between Verizon and Amazon is one example.

A Deeper Dive Into the Automotive Use Case

The automotive use case for edge computing is compelling, perhaps the most viable and commercially realistic application of the technology. To understand why I believe this to be the case, it is first helpful to clarify the myth of self-driving cars. Yes, self-driving cars are likely to become a reality in the coming decade or so. However, as naysayers like to point out, self-driving cars may never come into existence. Therefore, edge data centers for automotive use cases will never be built.

This is not a full or accurate viewpoint. Even if self-driving cars never materialize, there are many other connected vehicle technologies now in development and deployment. These will be the drivers of edge adoption, in my view.

The 5G Automotive Association (5GAA) is a sophisticated industry group whose members include the major car companies, electronics manufacturers, telcos, and other corporate stakeholders. The 5GAA is not the only entity dealing with connected vehicles, but it is the most prominent. Their views and publications are worth noting when it comes to predicting the future of edge data centers and connected vehicles.

The overall category dealt with by the 5GAA and its member companies is known as *Vehicle-to-Anything* (V2X) connectivity. The premise of V2X is that vehicles will have many different needs to connect to telco infrastructure and other digital services. These fall into three broad categories: connected driver warning, connective driver assistance, and connected cooperative driving. Some features in these categories are already in effect, such as speed limit notifications. Many more are planned to be phased in over the next decade.

With connective driver warning, for example, the 5GAA (based on member input) projects that we will see have V2X features like local hazard and traffic information, basic safety notifications, intersection safety notifications, and vulnerable road user awareness alerts in coming years.

Connected driver assistance may introduce V2X features like data collection and sharing for high-definition maps and automated valet parking. Many anticipated V2X features involve collective or cooperative driving scenarios. For instance, multiple cars on the road could engage in what the 5GAA calls *Cooperated Adaptive Cruise Control* or *Dynamic Cooperative Traffic Control.*

Making such V2X features work will require rich, fast connectivity for vehicles and edge computing instances. It will require, most likely, a large number of edge data centers deployed at frequent intervals along the road. In order to realize the function of cooperated adaptive cruise control, for example, all the cars involved in the cooperation must have ultra-low latency connections to servers that will handle the coordination and real-time vehicle feedback.

The connectivity requirements are self-evident, but so are the commercial possibilities for V2X and edge data centers. One of the most frequent and serious objections to the notion of pervasive edge computing and widely deployed edge data centers is, "Who will pay for this?" With automotive, the answer is obvious. The car business is massive. The two biggest car companies, Volkswagen and Toyota, have combined revenues of over half a trillion dollars. If car makers want to add a *Connectivity Package* option for cars, that could generate the funding needed to build edge data centers to support V2X.

CHAPTER 2

Drivers of the Edge Computing Revolution

The previous chapter offered an introduction to the concept of edge computing. It explored the *what* of edge computing—what it is and how it works. This chapter is about the *why*. It looks at why edge computing is experiencing growth and investment. In my view, there are three drivers of edge computing: technical, business, and societal/cultural.

These drivers will likely interact in an iterative, synergistic process, wherein breakthroughs in one area will affect the others. For example, as employees become accustomed to working from home, businesses are responding with new services that make such remote work more effective and secure. This, in turn, begets new cycles of technology development.

Technological Drivers

Technology trends make the growth of edge computing highly probable, if not inevitable. The first factor to consider is the projected growth of connected devices in the world. Current research finds that there are approximately 14 billion IoT devices and 16 billion smartphones/smart devices in use. Based on projected growth rates, and allowing for slowing of growth over time, this current installed base of 30 billion devices will grow to around 76 billion by 2032 and 137 billion within a decade after that—a 4.5× increase in 20 years. Figure 2.1 depicts these growth trajectories.

If I turn out to be wrong, please contact me in 2042 and let me know. I'll be pushing 80 but will, for sure, still be a major player in edge computing. Seriously, while no one can predict precisely what's coming, it appears likely that we will be seeing substantial growth in connected devices worldwide.

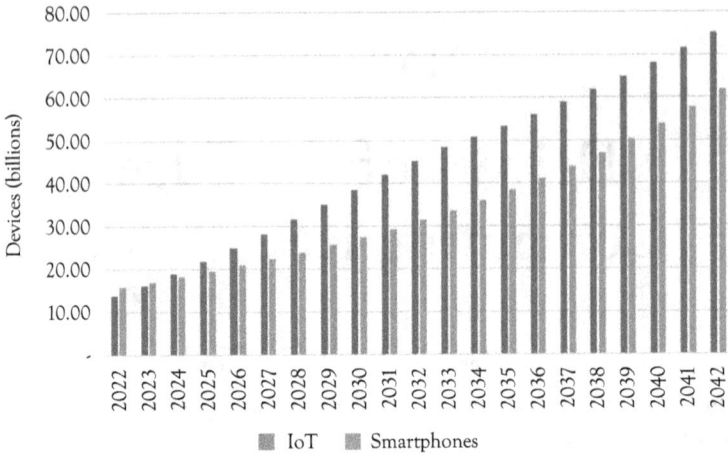

Figure 2.1 Smartphone/smart device and IoT device growth projections, based on data from IoTAnalytics.com and Statista

These devices will need to interact with compute and storage infrastructure. In some cases, the interaction will have to be ultra-low latency or real time in nature. That requirement will make widespread edge computing points of presence (PoPs) necessary. In other cases, the device owners will prefer not to transmit data to core data centers. They have this preference due to constraints in processing times. Or, they may not want to pay for the bandwidth.

It may turn out that these predictions are overly modest. Industry is only just beginning to see the potential in IoT. We could be measuring IoT and IIoT devices by the trillion in 2042.

5G is deploying in parallel. Although the technology has had a slow start in certain areas, due partly to a chicken-and-egg problem with applications, networks, and devices, it is clearly taking hold. 5G has greater antenna density and data transmission speeds than 4G. These characteristics are further technological drivers of edge computing. As users come to expect the latency that is possible with high antenna density and fast data transmission, service providers will need to install edge computing PoPs to deliver the expected latency.

Plus, it is useful to consider that 5G is really just the start of a trend. Within the next decade, we will likely see the emergence of 6G ... followed by 7G and on and on. These new generations of wireless connectivity will deliver greater and greater antenna density and data

Figure 2.2 The corner of Amsterdam Avenue and 100th Street in New York City: 1900 and today (Museum of the City of New York/ Google Street View)

transmission speeds. The world isn't going to become less connected and less demanding of high-performance mobility over time. The opposite is true. The world will expect ever-better mobile experiences and IoT device performance.

Pervasive edge computing seems to be the only way that these needs will be met, in technological terms. While it's impossible to predict the future, it seems clear that a major change in Internet infrastructure is approaching at the edge. As a fan of old photos of my hometown of New York, I like to say, "It's always 1900 someplace." Figure 2.2 shows the same street corner, Amsterdam Avenue, and 100th Street, as it looked in 1900 versus today. Back then, much of upper Manhattan was still farm-land. Today, it's one of the busiest and most densely populated areas in the world.

You might think, wow, what if I owned that farm back then? I'd be rich today! I believe that we will look back at edge development the same way we compare the corner of Amsterdam and 100th Street. It will seem inevitable that the buildup was coming. The question is, who will act on this opportunity?

Business Drivers

Businesses want new technologies to help them compete and grow. They exploit new technology developments to create new lines of business or increase income in existing areas of operation. As devices and edge PoPs proliferate, businesses are poised to drive growth in edge infrastructure and data center deployment.

Telecommunications companies, for example, want to build busi-nesses based on edge computing. In particular, they want to make the most of big investments in 5G. It is early in the lifecycle of data and computing service offerings in 5G, but they are coming on the market now. Some of these are simply faster service levels for user experiences that involve computing, such as games and mobile Internet use. Telcos are starting to offer edge data services, too, including MEC services, that give business customers access to an edge data center PoP.

Telco edge businesses are still somewhat embryonic at this point, but some stakeholders in the telco space want to build out RAN infrastruc-ture that includes edge data centers, and then make it available to firms that provide gaming experiences, stock trading, and the like. The working theory here is that telcos have a core competency in building networks but not necessarily in devising and delivering specialized service offer-ings for their customers. They will profit by becoming a sales channel, in effect, for other businesses working at the edge.

Changes in employee behavior and workplace norms are also busi-ness factors driving potential growth in edge data center deployment. The COVID-19 pandemic led to a huge increase in remote work. Now that the pandemic has subsided, many companies are still letting workers to stay home if they choose. This is known as *hybrid work*. Not everyone likes this idea, but the truth is that hybrid work is a fact of life in today's business.

To support hybrid work, companies are examining ways to bring applications and data closer to end users. This may involve the use of the new secure access service edge (SASE) model, which enables remote users to log into corporate digital assets without requiring them to go all the way to the corporate network to do so. It's a bit too complicated to get into detail here, but SASE favors the presence of edge data centers. The goal is to cut down on latency when interacting with enterprise software and virtual desktop infrastructure (VDI).

Digital transformation (DX) is another paradigm that augurs well for the growth of edge computing. DX is an umbrella term that describes a range of IT initiatives aimed at rethinking the relationships between companies, their customers, and suppliers. The idea is that digital technology can transform the way people interact with a brand. For example, a DX project might set out to make shopping more mobile-friendly.

Or, DX might establish an *omnichannel* marketing and sales relationship with the customer. In this approach, the customer can interact with a business over the Web, over the phone, through a mobile app, an in-store kiosk, and so forth. Multiple channels are open to the customer, versus the traditional single channel mode of engagement, such as visiting the store or calling an order line.

DX does not require edge computing, but edge latencies can certainly help DX be a success. If the goal is to transform customer engagement, then an ultra-fast user experience on a mobile app would be a big plus. For a retailer, this might mean installing closet-sized edge data centers at store locations.

A DX initiative might also blend into IoT. For example, a maker of tractors could install soil and atmospheric sensors on a tractor, and then engage with customers by sharing data about their farmland. They might integrate data feeds from orbiting satellites to enrich the data analytics for farming customers. In theory, delivering helpful agricultural data would be seen as a value-add by the farmer. Such a use case would favor edge data centers near farming sites.

Societal/Cultural Drivers

Some of the drivers of growth in edge computing will be societal or cultural in nature. As edge computing starts to power more use cases, end users will start to expect their availability and performance as a given in their daily lives. This, in turn, will push businesses to deliver on these implicit promises.

This is an exercise in predicting the future, so it's fraught with risk. Whatever I say now will probably seem laughable as events unfold, but if past history is any guide, we will likely see the following types of scenarios unfold: Consumers might expect to be in a metaverse while riding on a train. The experience will evolve from a novel treat to a daily expectation of service. If the metaverse isn't working for train riders, that will negatively affect the metaverse's brand.

Consumers might start to expect to get pizza delivery by drone in 15 minutes or less. They might expect videoconferencing on airplanes, and on and on. Since the 1990s, we have seen many exciting new technologies quickly turn into normalized, even boring requirements of daily living. Think about same-day package delivery from Amazon. That would have sounded like magic in 2001. Now, if we don't get it, we become irritated.

The culture shifts as technology enables new experiences. Edge computing and the technology use cases it enables will almost certainly be subject to the same forces. It will power new ways of living that consumers will come to expect. This, in turn, will drive vendors to build more edge data centers and related edge infrastructure.

Regulatory and Security Drivers

A number of laws prohibit companies from storing data outside of their domains. In health care, for example, the Health Insurance Portability and Accountability Act of 1996 (HIPAA) requires health care organizations to store patient information only in facilities they own. It is a violation of HIPAA to store medical records in the cloud.

As a result, health care organizations have to install sufficient computing and storage infrastructure to support this requirement. They build large, centralized data centers, which may be economically advantageous, but which may also slow down health care workflows as bandwidth constraints add processing time to patient care procedures.

The health care organization has the option of deploying computing hardware and software to remote locations to mitigate the bandwidth issue. The challenge has traditionally been to do this economically. Buying equipment and supporting it in remote locations has tended to be costly. The edge data center, with remote management, offers a solution. More on this concept in a moment.

Data sovereignty regulations pose a similar problem. In many European Union (EU) nations, for example, regulations mandate that personal information about citizens of a particular country remain in that country. Thus, if a German bank has a branch office in France, it cannot store data about French citizens on a server hosted inside German territory. Maintaining data sovereignty in the 27 EU member states can be quite a challenge. Edge data centers enable companies to keep data local to the country where it needs to be.

Even without regulations, concerns about data privacy and security drive interest in edge data centers. While smart people have differing opinions on this issue, the idea of storing sensitive information on multitenant cloud servers makes some security managers nervous. One could argue that this is not a legitimate concern, that in fact a cloud service like AWS has far superior security to that of the average bank. But, the assurance of control is much stronger when the bank owns the hardware it uses to store its data. This favors edge data centers.

Latency Versus *Data Gravity* and the Decentralized Enterprise

One current dialogue that reveals the immaturity of the edge category, as well as its potential for growth, is the debate over whether interest in the edge has anything to do with latency at all. The prevailing consensus in the IT industry is that edge computing is about latency. However, not everyone holds this viewpoint.

Denis Vilfort, Chief Story Teller and Director of Business Development at Hewlett Packard Enterprise (HPE), makes a persuasive argument that at least some adoption of edge data centers will be driven by what he calls *data gravity*, not latency. According to Vilfort, a wide variety of businesses want and need computing and storage in remote locations to handle the data that's being generated at those sites. That will require edge data centers.

For example, Vilfort offers the case of a company that operates 16 sawmills. Each sawmill uses multiple high-speed digital cameras for the purposes of quality assurance and coordination of the mill's equipment. These cameras generate 400 frames of digital images every second. Specialized software analyzes each frame to make sure that the mill is producing products of sufficient quality—and prevent employees from being hit in the head by logs traveling at 150 miles per hour through the production line.

As you can imagine, these cameras generate an enormous amount of data. This data has to be processed in real time, a function that is not possible with cloud-based computing. By the time the data goes to a cloud computing instance, gets analyzed, and data from the software comes back to the mill's operational systems, too much time will have elapsed for the cameras to do their jobs. There could be a lapse in quality or an industrial accident.

Bandwidth is the culprit. "You can create a million gallons of data, so to speak, and send it to the cloud through a straw," Vilfort said. He added:

> To understand why you need an edge data center in that sawmill, you have to compare the data you have to the time requirements for handling it. If you need the data onsite, you have data gravity. The data has to stay where it's created if it's to do what it needs to do.

To deal with its data gravity, the mill deploys edge data centers near the cameras, with fast connections linking the cameras with storage and computing capacity. In this case, that means 100-gigabit ethernet inside the mill itself. These computers are able to handle the camera data in real time.

What Vilfort is describing is sometimes called *the distributed enterprise.* This vision of enterprise computing posits that data gravity and other factors will make it optimal for corporations to deploy more computing and storage to remote locations. A distributed enterprise contrasts with the centralized approach taken by many enterprises today, wherein IT infrastructure is concentrated in on-premises data centers, colocation facilities, and cloud platforms.

You might think, "Well, what's new about that?" Enterprises have deployed servers and storage to remote locations for a generation. True, the deployment pattern is not novel. The sawmill does not have to install an edge data center. They might have a server room they can use for the necessary computer and storage equipment.

There are several problems with the traditional practice of deploying computers and storage to remote locations. This approach requires people on staff at those remote locations to manage and support the equipment. Their work includes installing and updating software in whatever technology *stack* the company runs on its servers.

It's an expensive proposition. And, it's getting increasingly difficult to find people who have the skills to do the work who are willing to situate themselves in remote locations. If you're an experienced VMware admin, for example, a sawmill in the wilds of Alberta may not be your first choice of a job site.

The modern edge data center offers a solution. An edge data center offers the factory a new way to manage the equipment. The edge data center is self-contained and can be entirely remotely managed. The factory can take advantage of a new system architecture, management model, and IT operational economics.

While not a maintenance-free piece of infrastructure, the edge data center reduces the on-site admin workload significantly. The software support aspects of its administration can be handled almost 100 percent remotely. New generations of system management, such as HPE Greenlake software, make this possible.

Additionally, it is now also possible to overcome the traditional financial obstacles to this model. Until recently, if you wanted to install servers, storage, and networking hardware in a remote location, you had to buy it. That is a capital expense (CapEx), which means using up cash or borrowing money to finance equipment purchases.

Plus, you had to buy enough capacity to allow for growth. For instance, if your digital cameras generate a terabyte of data every day, then you would need to buy enough storage to hold at least 750 terabytes over the three-year lifecycle of the storage hardware. In Year one, you'd store 250 terabytes, but leave 500 terabytes empty, even though you paid for them.

The economics of the distributed enterprise are a turnoff for some corporations. They don't like big CapEx outlays. Nor do they like the idea of overbuying in anticipation of future capacity needs. It's not an insurmountable problem, but it impedes the implementation of the distributed enterprise model.

HPE is pioneering a new approach to infrastructure procurement that solves the CapEx problem. They have a program whereby the customer can pay for hardware as needed, much as in a cloud computing relationship. Instead of CapEx, with its implied overbuying, the HPE relationship offers an *as-a-service* mode of paying for hardware on an operating expense (OpEx) basis. This is quite attractive for some financial managers.

HPE has also addressed a related administrative issue, which is the custom configuration of numerous *stacks* to work across a number of sites and clusters. The company can ship equipment to remote locations with sophisticated combinations of operating system and application software preinstalled.

The HPE approach, and those like it, enable corporations to run a distributed enterprise without the CapEx hurdle and the requirement to staff remote data centers. They can run most of the sites remotely. The economics are like those available in the cloud, but the system performance is far better.

CHAPTER 3

Conceptualizing the Edge Data Center

What is an edge data center? Surprisingly, or perhaps not surprisingly, a definition of this basic unit of edge computing has been difficult to establish. For some stakeholders, an edge data center must be a miniature replica of a hyperscale facility, with all of the same functionality. For others, a server in a closet qualifies as an edge data center. Are both definitions acceptable? I'm going to attempt to resolve this conflict. There's no argument quite like the argument between tech professionals nerding out on their favorite paradigms, but I'm a peacemaker.

One reason for disagreement on this issue is the multisector nature of the edge computing space. Telecom companies see the edge one way. Big data center providers see it another. Car companies have their views, and so forth. It can be hard to achieve consensus on what an edge data center looks like and what it does. This chapter will endeavor to define the edge data center in a way that will please most stakeholders, or at least make sense to them.

The Issue of Size

Discussions about edge data centers can get confusing right out of the gate if people aren't clear about the size of the facility they envision. The range of sizes being contemplated for edge data centers goes from rack enclosures with a 6U capacity, which is about the size of a small refrigerator, to 50,000-square-foot purpose-built facilities that have the floor space of the average supermarket. A U consists of 1.75 inches of vertical data center rack space. Computer hardware is manufactured in Us. You can see servers listed as 1U, 4U, and so forth.

Obviously, there are huge differences in computing capacity, energy consumption, and cost at the two ends of the spectrum. Most of this book is focused on the smaller side of the scale. However, it's useful to achieve clarity on what size of edge data center is in the works. Deploying a 6U rack enclosure is quite a different project from constructing a 50,000-square-foot building.

Current Approaches to Edge Data Center Design

The data center industry, including makers of computer cabinets, is coming to market with a wide variety of edge data center designs. There is already an impressive number of options. The selection will likely grow as time goes on. The following is a rundown of today's leading approaches to edge data center design. Figure 3.1 offers an overview.

A Purpose-Built Structure

Some companies are building edge data centers as purpose-built structures. They are constructing a building of suitable size to hold whatever edge computing capacity they require and installing server

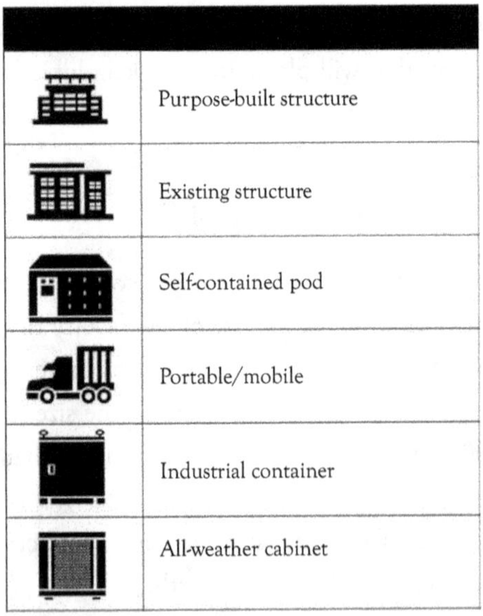

	Purpose-built structure
	Existing structure
	Self-contained pod
	Portable/mobile
	Industrial container
	All-weather cabinet

Figure 3.1 Current approach to edge data center design

racks, cooling equipment, and power backup equipment. The advantage to this approach is that the owner can design it for their exact requirements. If you need 16 42U racks and 150 kilowatts, with a biometric security system, that's precisely what you'll get. The downside is cost and repeatability. This is an expensive route to take if you need to build, say, a 1,000 such sites.

A Data Center in an Existing Structure

In this approach, the owner can place a data center in a building that wasn't designed to be a data center. For example, if you have a vacant floor in an office building, you could bring in your server racks and cooling systems and set up a small edge data center. This is not too different from the traditional *server room* that predominated in the precloud era. For financial services companies, such setups have long been the norm. They want computing to be as near to the trading floor as possible.

The limitations in this model have to do with structural issues and the availability of electrical power. Most buildings were not built to support fully loaded server racks, which can place up to 5,000 pounds of weight in a six square feet of floor space. That could cause the floor to collapse. And, most buildings are not designed for the kind of power and cooling required for even a small data center.

With the edge, what may be the most likely use of this approach will be the conversion of small utility buildings near cell towers into micro data centers. Or, a cell tower company might adapt a building close to the tower to serve as a data center.

The Self-Contained Pod

In the last few years, a number of innovative companies have developed edge data centers in self-contained pods. These vary in size and specification, but two examples offer a glimpse of what's available on the market. Figure 3.2 shows the RakworX modular data center, which is available in a range of sizes. It can hold up to 10 52U racks and support up to 350 kW of power in its IT load. It functions as a complete data center, with a secure entrance, server racks, and built-in cooling.

Figure 3.2 RakworX modular data center, which can hold up to 10 52U racks

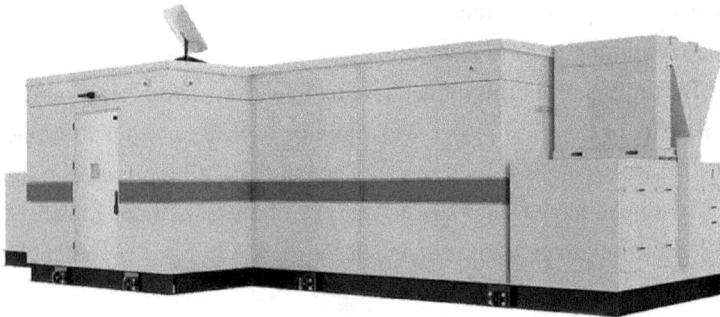

Figure 3.3 Compass data centers' Quantum modular 100 kW data center

Figure 3.3 shows the Quantum modular data center, made by Compass Data Centers, an established builder of hyperscale facilities. This unit can support up to 100 kW of IT load. This translates into 12 full-sized racks. It is 48 feet by 12 feet inside. The pod is designed for rugged outdoor use. It features ballistic materials that can withstand hurricanes with 160-mile-per-hour winds or even gunfire.

Both of these designs require some sort of permanent base for installation. This might be a concrete pad or a location inside a building. They also need to be surrounded by a security fence or comparable barrier.

The Portable Micro Data Center

Some edge cases require the temporary presence of an edge data center. Examples include oil and gas production, seasonal agriculture, and military deployments. For these uses, a portable edge data center might be the best option. Figure 3.4 shows one such example. It is made by RakworX. In this case, they have built a full data center that can go on a 53-foot road trailer. The trailer also carries a powerful electrical generator to keep the equipment and cooling systems running.

All-Weather Cabinets

Some edge data centers are going to be adaptations of all-weather cabinets used in existing electrical and telecommunications workloads. For example, an Nvent/Hoffman ComLine Vertical Mount Cabinet can hold a 6U rack. It's designed to be mounted on a telephone pole. A 6U rack is small, but for certain edge computing situations, such as remote IoT management, it might be more than adequate.

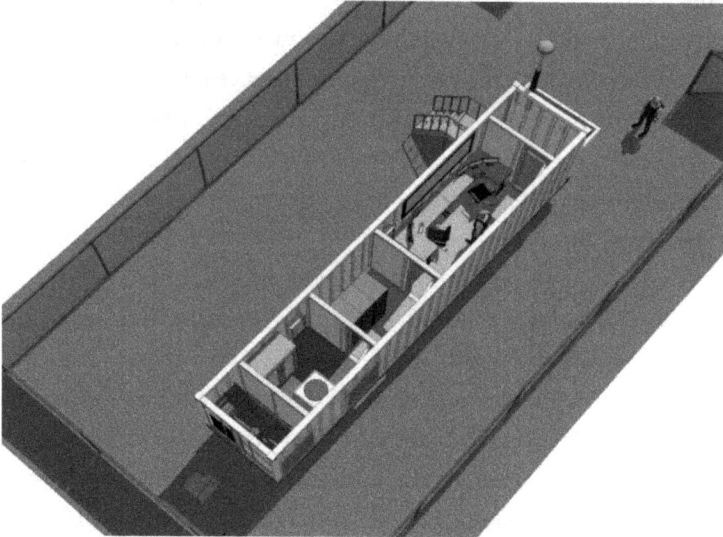

Figure 3.4 Interior of mobile data center in a 53-inch trailer built by RakworX

Industrial Container Modules

Indoor and industrial edge computing scenarios may make existing computer containers serve as edge data centers. For example, the Chatsworth Products RMR Modular can hold a rack up to 47U inside. For an industrial facility, that could support more than enough computer hardware for their edge computing needs. Schneider Electric also manufactures a range of such enclosures.

Is It a Data Center or Edge Compute Instance?

Some of these edge data centers are small-scale replicas of traditional data centers. They have doors that lock, security systems and private, enclosed server racks you can walk up to and administer. They have, in industry parlance, *power, ping, and pipe,* referring to electrical power, a network connection that *pings* and air conditioning *pipe.* Others are basically just equipment cabinets. Does an equipment cabinet qualify as a data center? It depends on whom you ask.

For a veteran data center manager, the idea that a steel cabinet hanging from a telephone pole qualifies as a data center is frankly an insult to their professionalism. How dare you! That metal box is not a data center … or is it? I'm bringing this up because I believe the edge should make everyone rethink their definition of a data center.

Here is my attempt at defining an edge data center: *An edge data center is a dedicated space or container that holds computer, storage, and networking hardware functioning in the service of an edge computing use case.* The form factors will vary.

An edge data center is also about more than just hardware and the container that holds it together. In my view, an edge data center must also run software that makes it function like a data center. This would include applications for server, network, and storage administration, just like a full-size data center. In an edge data center, this software would almost always be for a remote administrator, though the edge data center should also enable an admin to modify configurations and install software physically.

The presence of data center management software distinguishes the edge data center from a simple computing instance in a noncore location.

Thus, the server in the closet may not qualify as an edge data center if it's just doing something like running the company e-mail system. That's not an edge data center.

An edge data center should be part of a bigger environment, though I would not consider this an absolute parameter to qualify as an edge data center. There may be standalone edge data centers, but my sense is that most edge data centers will be deployed as part of an edge system of some kind—with centralized management.

Connectivity is part of the picture, too. An edge data center will feature connections to networks that support its use case. It may be plugged into the public Internet, a 5G telecom network, or an SD-WAN. It might have a satellite hookup or be part of a private 5G network.

Edge data centers should also have ways to manage their power and cooling requirements. Same for security. The site, or unit, has to have built-in security countermeasures to prevent physical and cyber threats from disrupting its operation. These are further arguments against including the *server in the closet* as an edge data center.

One thing to keep in mind in this discussion is that power capacity and physical size do not always correlate. In general, the greater the power capacity of a data center, the larger it is, but *density* can affect this relationship. Certain types of equipment use more power in a smaller form factor than others. A rack full of such hardware has greater density, in terms of power consumption. Thus, a rack that ordinarily supports equipment that uses 8 kW might now use 12 kW.

High device density can be problematic in terms of cooling. Integrated circuits are like toasters. The more electricity they use, the hotter they get. Placing too many circuits too close together may generate heat at levels that can damage the hardware. Indeed, if a rack gets hot enough, the circuits may melt, or even catch fire.

The Common Denominator: Provisioning the Edge Stack

Whatever the form factor, the common denominator of all these edge data centers is the requirement to house the client's distinctive technology stack. There is no universal edge technology stack. The Linux Foundation and other standards bodies are working on developing standards for edge operating systems, but for now, each organization deploying at the edge will have its own preferred stack.

The stack will depend on what kind of *shop* is installing the edge data center. For example, a *VMware shop* will use the ESXI hypervisor to run its virtual machines at the edge. A *Nutanix shop* will need Nutanix operating software, and so forth. For each of these, there will then be any number of customizations, such as the requirement to run Kubernetes. HPE's Denis Vilfort likens this to baking a cake with layers. Each client will have its own unique layer cake.

Someone will be responsible for baking the cakes, so to speak, in the provisioning process for edge technology stacks. This remains an open area, with some organizations doing the work manually, while others have semi- or fully automated systems for provisioning operating systems, hypervisors, and the like at the edge. To some, the edge technology provisioning process represents an opportunity to profit from improving the way it's done.

CHAPTER 4

Hasn't This Problem Already Been Solved?

One of the classic putdowns you hear in the venture world is that a new technology is a *solution in search of a problem.* Someone dreams up a new idea, only to find that the problem it purports to solve has already been addressed. Or, it becomes obsolete so quickly that it becomes truly a solution in search of a problem.

This was the case with the long-forgotten FlashPix digital image format, which was developed jointly by Kodak, Microsoft, and Hewlett Packard in 1995. It created multiple resolutions of an image that enabled faster transmission over networks with limited bandwidth, such as dial-up Internet. It was a good idea, for 1992, but rapid improvements in bandwidth made it obsolete upon its debut.

You will meet people who believe edge computing falls into this category. I am not going to say they are entirely wrong, because it's wise to listen to critics of a new technology concept. (As my old boss once said, "God forbid, you might learn something....") However, given that a lot of smart people and successful companies are investing effort and money into edge data centers, that would seem to be an argument that edge computing is a solution to a problem, rather than a solution seeking a problem.

Still, it is worth reviewing the existing alternatives to edge data center deployment, with the goal of understanding how they do, and don't address the issues of latency and data transmission. These include hyperscalers, CDNs, urban data centers, cloud providers, and colocation companies.

Edge Versus Hyperscalers and Corporate Data Centers

Some corporations have sufficiently massive computing and device connectivity needs that they can justify building their own hyperscale data centers. The big tech firms certainly fall into this category, with companies like Google, Apple, and Facebook erecting numerous hyperscale facilities. Does an operator of hyperscale data centers need edge data centers to function at the edge? Isn't the presence of a hyperscale data center enough?

The answer is that it depends on where that hyperscale data center is located. In certain locations, the hyperscale data center will be close enough to end users that it can deliver ultra-low latency. However, given the tendency of hyperscalers to build on cheap land outside of urban areas, much of the time the data center will not be able to deliver the latency required. And, hyperscale data centers are not generally set up to address location-specific use cases. Their management platforms are not typically set up to align end user location with service delivery, a key factor in edge computing.

Edge Versus Branch Office Network Equipment

Branch offices and retail locations often house some computing and storage capacity that's part of their network equipment. If you go to the back office in a big box store, for example, you will invariably see some sort of server rack or comparable setup. This hardware is there to help the store process its point-of-sale (PoS) cash register data and related workloads.

Is the branch office *network closet*, to speak, an edge data center? The answer is that it probably could be, but it's a matter of software. The necessary hardware might be present. It's in the right location to serve end user devices. However, the equipment alone doesn't deliver edge computing.

To be an edge data center, the hardware at the location has to be configured to be an edge PoP. The exact parameters of this configuration are evolving, but the assumption is that it will include remote management for edge services, monitoring of edge performance, and more.

Edge Versus CDNs

As previously mentioned, today's CDNs are already delivering edge computing services to millions of devices. They've been at it for over 20 years. Akamai Technologies, for example, is a multibillion-dollar CDN operator that offers, in the words of its website, to "Run code at the edge, just milliseconds away from your users."

Akamai runs over 300,000 edge PoPs around the world. So, given that impressive achievement, why are we even talking about edge data centers? The answer is that for all of that presence, Akamai does not (yet) have a monopoly on edge computing. And, Akamai and its fellow CDNs are still not fully positioned to deliver ultra-low latency wherever it's needed. Akamai's edge PoPs are mostly located inside telecom carrier facilities. This is good and bad for them, in my view. It has been an outstanding strategy, but it still puts them too far away from end users much of the time.

CDNs also do not address the other edge use case, which involves data transmission. Organizations that deploy edge data centers are often doing it to avoid moving data back and forth from the core. That is not supported by CDNs, which deliver data to end users, not the other way around. This may change, of course, but currently, CDNs are not a replacement for distributed edge data centers. However, CDNs may be in the best position to dominate the emerging edge computing industry. They're already more than halfway there.

Edge Versus Small Urban Data Centers

In the average city, you can find quite a few small data centers in operation. These might be old *server rooms* in buildings housing financial firms or data centers set up to support some local industry. Assuming they are on the right fiber connections, these sites can definitely support ultra-low latency and short-range data transmission use cases for devices within a defined geographic radius. Does that make them edge data centers? Like the hyperscale example, the answer depends on how they are configured. Without the right management software and other functional parameters, a local data center cannot automatically serve edge computing workloads.

Edge Versus Public Cloud Platforms

The big three public cloud platform providers, AWS, Microsoft Azure, and Google Cloud Platform (GCP), do not deliver edge computing services through their core facilities. Indeed, it is against the AWS/Azure/GCP model that edge computing is most often compared. This is not to knock them. These platforms have transformed the world of IT. However, they typically do not come anywhere near the latency envisioned for effective edge computing. Their hyperscale facilities are almost always geographically remote from end users. In fact, their locations are often deliberately obscured from end users, to prevent malicious physical interference with the hardware. Moving data in and out of those data centers tends to be costly and time consuming. The major cloud platforms are addressing this issue. AWS, for example, now offers local zones to supplement its core zones.

Edge Versus Colocation Service Providers

Colocation service providers operate numerous, geographically distributed data centers. This puts them in a good position to be edge computing service providers. Their business model, which involves customized deployment of hardware and software based on clients' needs, further enhances their ability to support edge use cases. The issue for the current state of colocation is geographic presence.

Some colocation facilities are geographically suitable to support edge models. The enormous Switch facility in Las Vegas, for example, can deliver very low latency to users in most parts of that city. However, it cannot do the same for users who connect to Switch from more distant places.

Like the cloud platforms, colocation providers are now in too few locations to be effective edge providers. This is likely to change, as colocation companies build more edge capacity. I suspect the colocation providers will take the lead in the nascent edge industry.

Edge Versus SD-WAN Providers

Companies that provide SD-WAN service do not automatically support edge computing. However, they are in an excellent position to add edge computing to their business models. They are already connecting remote locations with core data centers. They have network equipment distributed throughout these locations. It would not be a big step to add edge data centers to their infrastructures. This is starting to happen, but it is still quite early in the process.

Edge Versus Device Clusters

One of the more intriguing ideas to emerge from dialogues about the future of edge computing has to do with skipping the creation of edge centers altogether—and letting the massive installed base of mobile devices serve as edge computing instances for each other. This is not as crazy as it sounds. There are nearly 120 million iPhones in use the United States right now.[1] Each device could, in theory, offer nearly instant data processing for another nearby device. The phone is, after all, a small computer. It is probable that some version of this concept will come into existence as edge computing becomes more prevalent.

[1] Statista—Number of iPhone users in the United States from 2012 to 2022.

CHAPTER 5

Edge Computing Deployment

Edge computing is early enough in its technology lifecycle that this chapter will likely become obsolete rather quickly. Indeed, some of this is speculation, but that is normal when multiple industries grapple with a new way of using IT. No one knows for sure what is about to happen. However, it makes sense to develop scenarios and assess how they will affect customers and suppliers alike.

To get a sense of how edge computing will be deployed in the field, it is first useful to think through how the edge will evolve as a business model. Some edge computing instances will be wholly owned and operated by businesses. Others will be leased to customers in a variety of arrangements. How this will all happen is certain to be different from what I'm positing here, but hopefully this will serve as an instructive thought exercise.

The Edge as an IT Department Responsibility

It is likely that a sizable portion of edge computing instances will be directly owned and controlled by corporations. Their deployment and management will be the responsibility of those companies' respective IT departments or outsource vendors. Examples include IoT networks and the distributed enterprise model described in Chapter 2.

In such cases, the edge data center customer and supplier are one and the same. There is no commercial relationship between the two. That said, a company may engage in internal chargebacks for use of edge data centers, but as a business, it's a closed loop.

The Edge as a Business Model

Businesses are starting to capitalize on the edge as a business model. It's early, and there have already been several notable failures as startups attempted to create businesses by building edge data centers and finding tenants for them. The approaches are starting to gel, nonetheless.

One model is to build edge data centers and lease their capacity to clients. This is a version of the standard colocation business, and in some cases, it is established colo providers that are pioneering the model. At this moment, it seems like the *build it and they will come approach* does not work. Demand is not strong or broad enough to make this model work. A *build to suit* style seems more viable.

The client gets the option of renting edge capacity on per-kilowatt basis. Thus, a 100-kW edge data center might rent 10 kW to one client and 90 to another. The client could also rent by the rack, or the *U*, and so forth.

The edge cloud represents an alternative business model. In this approach, the edge computing provider makes virtual machines available in specific edge locations. This model offers the flexibility advantages of cloud computing, but with the benefits of locating at the edge.

Another possible variant could be the merging of an existing, unrelated business with edge computing. For example, a business with multiple locations, like an electric utility or a chain of gas stations, could make its sites available to edge computing customers. Walmart has indicated it may follow this strategy, allocating space in its more than 3,000 stores to data centers.[1] This would provide them with added revenue on existing real estate. This might be a natural move for Amazon. Deploying edge data centers to Whole Foods Markets could put them instantly into a lot of attractive edge locations.

Modes of Edge Deployment

With these business models in mind, let's turn to the possible ways one can deploy edge computing capacity. The following is not an exhaustive

---

[1] N. Sarah. December 21, 2019. "Walmart's Secret Weapon to Fight Off Amazon: The Supercenter," *The Wall Street Journal.*

list. Rather, it's a glimpse of the high-level options that are emerging in the edge computing market.

Industrial/Enterprise

Corporations now use edge data centers to provide computing and data storage in remote locations where the cloud is impractical. In this distributed enterprise use case, the ability to handle large amounts of data locally is more important than latency. Though deployment processes will vary by organization, the most likely scenario is that IT departments will set up edge data centers and administer them centrally with whatever infrastructure management tools they currently use.

For example, if a business uses VMware data center management solutions or HPE Greenlake to install and manage servers in its main data centers and cloud instances, it will most likely use these technologies for its edge sites. The edge data center becomes just another data center location they are managing with these solutions. It would not make sense to adopt a separate infrastructure management technology to handle the edge.

Colocation

A colocation provider can set up an edge data center and make it available to customers as another location for hosting their IT infrastructure. For example, a colo provider might host its clients' infrastructure in large facilities in Virginia and Arizona. If the provider then builds edge sites in Los Angeles and San Francisco, it can invite its clients to deploy computing and storage to those edge sites.

The edge data center would simply be another geographic option for the colo provider's clients. The colo provider would manage the installation and support of those edge instances using whatever infrastructure management tools it normally uses in its operation.

Virtual Versus Bare Metal

Organizations that want to deploy edge computing instances can choose between *bare metal* or virtual hosting. With bare metal, the edge computing software is installed directly onto dedicated servers (the *metal*), which are under the exclusive control of the system owner. For example, with bare metal, you might install your software on a Dell server in an edge data center. You get to select the type of server, along with its characteristics and configuration. There are several advantages to the bare metal approach: You get complete control over the hardware. Only your data and applications are running on the server, so you don't have to worry as much about security issues or performance problems due to a *noisy neighbor* on a shared machine. The only downside is cost. It is far more expensive to deploy an exclusive, dedicated machine than it is to share hardware with a virtual machine (VM).

A VM, in contrast, can be one of several complete computer systems running on a shared piece of hardware. Using software known as a hypervisor, the physical server's computing capacity is split among the virtual machines it is hosting. Thus, a single Dell server could simultaneously run a Windows Server with MySQL, a Linux server with Postgres SQL, and so forth. Each VM *thinks* it is the only server running on the hardware. The VMs have no awareness of one another, and in theory, the data they handle is completely walled off from the other virtual machines.

There are a number of advantages to running VMs at the edge. Given the physical constraints of edge data centers, it makes economic sense to run as many compute instances as possible on whatever hardware can fit into the data center limited rack space. Bare metal, in contrast, can be highly inefficient, with hardware sitting idle or underutilized for long periods of time. As a result, virtual edge compute is almost always less expensive to run in comparison to bare metal.

In addition, virtual infrastructure tends to be more flexible, with system owners able to spin up or spin down VMs as needed—and avoid paying for them, which contrasts with the fixed rental rates that are typical with bare metal.

The downsides to virtual edge computing stem from possible performance issues and security risks. If one VM is running hot, with a high load of computing going on, that can crowd out the other VMs on the same hypervisor. The busy VM can hog the available bandwidth, further adding to latency for its neighbors. And, security can be an issue. There is always a risk of eavesdropping when two VMs share the same hypervisor.

Edge Cloud

Virtual edge infrastructure may take the form of an edge cloud. To understand what this means, keep in mind the fact that cloud computing is a software architecture first and a business model second. As a software architecture, the cloud involves abstracting the physical hardware required for computing from the software it's running. In a cloud architecture, software can be running pretty much anywhere … on a cloud, so to speak.

If you want to run Windows Server in the cloud, you use cloud management software to spin up a Windows Server instance. The software will proceed to create a VM running Windows Server for you on a physical server somewhere. You don't need to know, or indeed cannot know exactly where it is. You might have a general idea that the physical server running your Windows Server VM is located in Virginia, but that's all.

In practice, two forms of cloud computing currently predominate. The majority of cloud computing occurs on the big three public cloud platforms, which are AWS, Microsoft Azure, and Google Cloud Platform. However, it is also possible to run a private cloud, wherein you arrange for a cloud software architecture on your own privately controlled infrastructure, such as that which runs in on-premises data centers or colocation facilities. A private cloud combines the flexibility of cloud computing with the security and performance advantages of privately owned infrastructure.

With a private cloud, system owners can spin systems up and down as needed. What private clouds don't have is the public cloud's theoretically infinite capacity. AWS, Azure, and GCP have so much capacity that it's unlimited, in effect. A private cloud is always limited by its owner's level of investment.

Cloud computing offers a variety of benefits, mostly related to flexibility. Capacity is available on demand. The cloud provider handles the hard work of installing and supporting the hardware and cloud data centers. You also avoid the CapEx involved in building data centers and buying hardware. That said, the cloud is not as inexpensive as some might believe.

The reason I'm getting into this level of detail about cloud computing is to introduce the concept of the edge cloud, which has some similarities to today's public cloud, but also some notable differences. In an edge cloud, you get the benefits of abstraction. You don't have to worry about buying and installing the hardware or setting up edge data centers. You can spin up or spin down edge computing instances whenever you want. This type of on-demand edge infrastructure offers great flexibility and agility. It will almost certainly be less expensive than equivalent bare metal hosting at the edge.

Edge cloud differs from AWS or Azure in two profound ways, however. One relates to capacity. Edge data centers are small, so capacity will always have some hard limits. There is no bottomless well of compute and storage to tap into in an edge cloud. If there are 10 racks in a remote pod, you have 10 racks to fill, unless you deploy another pod. And, most importantly, edge cloud must address issues of location. With an edge cloud, you may get the advantage of flexible VM deployment, but unlike in a public cloud, where your system is running in a broad geographic zone, in an edge cloud, you have to know exactly where it is. That's the whole point.

Purpose-Built/Wholly Owned

We are likely to see the emergence of large-scale, purpose-built edge computing networks that serve the needs of a single owner. As of now, this is a guessing game, but you can imagine a major player like Meta building out a network of edge facilities to support its metaverse, or Apple creating edge PoPs for iPhone users, and so forth. Whatever these companies do, however, they will almost certainly find themselves dealing with all the same edge data center deployment challenges as everyone else. The difference is that Meta and Apple have more resources to master a rollout than most other companies on the scene.

How Will This Play Out? Drawing Conclusions From Emerging Modes of Deployment

As you can see, the edge right now presents a complicated picture. How will this play out? Who will *win* at the edge, at least in the beginning? One issue is that although it's useful to separate the various business models and modes of deployment for the sake of analysis, the emergence of the edge will probably involve hybrid, overlapping projects characterized by alliances between companies.

Gaining the competitive edge at the edge will require such extensive capital outlays—coupled with mastery of unfamiliar technologies—that even the biggest players will avoid going it alone. This is already starting to happen. In May 2022, Amazon and Verizon announced the launch of AWS Wavelength Zones in 19 metro areas in the United States.[2]

Amazon has the cloud computing platform and customers. Verizon has the telecom infrastructure, network, and expertise to manage the deployment of the edge PoPs that will make the Wavelength Zones a reality. Amazon doesn't want to get into the telco business. Verizon doesn't want to get into the cloud business. It's a natural fit.

Going a little deeper into the Wavelength Zone, you can perceive another layer of alliances supporting the endeavor. Verizon doesn't actually own the cell towers that will provide the 5G connectivity for users of the Wavelength Zones. Those are the province of tower companies like American Tower, Crown Castle, and many others. Verizon rents the towers from these companies. Additionally, the AWS cloud capacity that supports the Wavelength Zones is not all hosted in facilities directly owned by Amazon. AWS is a major tenant in data centers owned by digital REITs.

Amazon and Verizon shared that they envision this new edge infrastructure supporting "immersive VR gaming, video distribution, and connected and autonomous vehicles." According to their announcement, 75 percent of the U.S. population lives within 150 miles of a Wavelength

---

[2] Verizon.com. May 25, 2022. "Verizon and AWS Expand Edge Computing to 19 U.S. Metro Areas."

Zone. The clients are evidently companies like Meta. It will be interesting to see if the AWS Wavelength Zones are a commercial success. If they are, they will show how a complex synergy of major players can work in making the edge a business reality.

Envisioning Three Foundational Edge Businesses

Early as it may be, it is apparent that three foundational edge businesses are coming into existence. I see them like this:

- The telephonic edge—led by telcos and/or alliances like AWS Wavelength Zones, the telephonic edge is driven primarily by mobile device use cases.
- The enterprise edge—features exclusive enterprise deployments of edge computing in manufacturing, IoT, and related closed-loop use cases.
- The cloud/colo edge—driven by hosting requirements, with cloud and colo clients solving latency and data management challenges through edge deployments.

Edge Data Center Deployment Case Studies

What does an edge data center deployment look like in real life? I asked two experienced edge data center experts about their recent projects to get a sense of what's involved in taking an edge data center from plan to reality. Michael Siteman, a data center consultant, described what went into getting a modular datacenter built in a suburb of Los Angeles.

The first thing to understand is the network of contractual relationships that support an edge data center. These will be a little different every time, but in general, they follow a pattern. In Siteman's project, the following entities formed agreements to work together:

- The landlord, which owned the physical property on which the data center would be installed
- The data center owner/operator
- The builder of the prefabricated modular unit

- The data center owner/operator's client(s), that is, the data center's tenants
- The data center maintenance and support provider

The purpose of this project was to set up a backup instance for a major colocation client. The client was already hosting many of its digital assets in Arizona. It wanted the ability to host applications and data on a *failover* in a different geographic location. For a variety of reasons, they elected not to host this backup in an existing data center facility. They wanted their own, small, standalone edge data center.

Initially, Siteman identified a suitable vacant lot. It would be relatively easy to pour a concrete pad and install the modular data center. However, the city said no. The site was not zoned for that kind of use. So, they had to look elsewhere.

Siteman then found a building that had space to rent for the modular data center. The next step was to negotiate two agreements with the property owner. The first was a basic lease. However, the lease has to specify that the data center owner/operator has the right to install and operate a data center on the property. This may sound obvious, but it's a point to keep in mind. You cannot make assumptions about what a landlord will or will not allow in a building.

Siteman then negotiated a master services agreement (MSA) with the property owner. This was supplemental to the lease. It dealt with the property owner's obligations regarding the physical services, such as maintenance and repairs. For example, the property owner might agree to remove an obstacle that blocked access to the data center within four hours.

The challenge in negotiating the MSA comes from the chain of relationships that it affects. If an issue with the property impedes the operation of the data center, that will, in turn, affect the data center owner/operator and its service-level agreement (SLA) with the data center tenant. The SLA might specify a maximum time allowed to restore service in the event of an outage. The property MSA must align with the data center operator's SLA to its client.

Similarly, the service agreement with the data center maintenance and support company must also align with the data center operator's client

SLA. In the event of an outage, the support provider must agree to take required steps to bring the data center back online within an agreed-upon time window. This might involve *rolling trucks* to visit the site in person or undertake remote actions to restore service. The maintenance and support agreement will also specify how, and how quickly various steps will be taken to replace hardware, reboot servers, and the like.

It is then necessary to negotiate agreements with the fiber optic network provider and power company. These agreements, too, must specify service levels. For fiber, the SLA might identity minimum bandwidth speeds, as well as time-to-restore service in the event of an outage. The power purchase agreement will have similar characteristics. In some cases, the electrical power agreement will be part of the lease and property owner's MSA.

Siteman's team could then proceed with the actual physical deployment of the modular data center once all the parties to these various agreements have signed off on their commitments. He has to pull permits for pouring a concrete foundation and the electrical hookup, which is essentially permission to string 50 feet of copper wire from the electrical mains to a transformer. In his experience, these are not difficult permits to get, given that the law treats the modular data center as *personal property*, not a built structure. He doesn't need a construction permit to deploy the modular data center.

The modular data center, which has been constructed elsewhere and disassembled, was brought to the site on a truck and installed using a crane. It took about two weeks to fabricate it on the site, connect the power and fiber, and so forth. In Siteman's experience, the entire process of setting up the site and getting the data center deployed can take up to two months.

Ron Vokoun, who has been involved in data center construction for over 20 years, shared his experience deploying a prefabricated edge data center. The project started with a vacant lot, nothing but dirt. "It's much easier than traditional construction, in most cases," he explained. "If you're using the larger fabricators, they've got this all worked out." The trick, he said, is to work through inspection issues to avoid holdups and unexpected problems.

Vokoun's team worked with a fabricator that arranged for the data center module to be inspected by building inspectors in the location where it was manufactured—not where it was to be deployed. This process, which is common in situations that rely on prefabricated elements, involves state-licensed building inspectors certifying the prefabricated structure before it ships.

The unit arrives at its deployment site with a certificate from the out-of-state inspectors. Depending on the state, these out-of-state inspections are honored on a reciprocal basis. "You have to be sure you can do this," Vokoun added. "This is part of your due diligence. You don't want to go through the process of getting the unit certified in Colorado, for example, if inspectors in Virginia won't honor that inspection." As Vokoun has seen, the reciprocity of inspections can also be an issue at the local level. The municipality where the unit is being deployed also has to agree to honor the out-of-state inspection.

From there, the construction and deployment of process are relatively straightforward. The site has to be flattened and modified for drainage, much as it would in any other real estate project. This may involve adding gravel to the site. The contractor has to arrange for concrete slabs to be poured for the data center unit and generators, if those are part of the deployment. He or she must also build underground conduits for power and fiber hookups.

When the unit arrives, the contractor arranges for it to be attached to the slab. Subcontractors connect the power and fiber. "That's really all there is to it, in practical terms," Vokoun said. "If you've done your permit work properly, all you need at that point is to have an inspector sign off on the overall site. The process can move very quickly."

There can still be surprises, however. A fire marshal, for example, might want to inspect the site. This may be a welcome proposition, given the liability and negative publicity that can arise if a modular data center starts a wildfire.

CHAPTER 6

Connecting the Edge Data Center

An edge data center is connected in two directions. It has to have a fast connection to end users' devices. The data center must also have a fast connection to the Internet. Without these two sets of connections, the edge data center cannot fulfil its role in delivering low latency computing.

Connecting to Device Users

There are two basic modes of connection between an edge data center and end users' devices: wireless and wired. Wireless connections involve end user devices, such as mobile devices like smartphones and IoT sensors, communicating with the edge data center through built-in antennas on both ends. In a wired configuration, users' devices connect to the edge data center with cables. These might be part of an Ethernet LAN or some form of dedicated fiber network. Wired scenarios include office parks, factory floors, call centers, and financial trading locations.

Connecting to the Internet or Private Networks

The wired and wireless scenarios both require the edge data center to have a direct, high-speed connection to the Internet or some equivalent private network. In a closed LAN connection, such as those used on factory floors, the edge data center can connect to internal, privately owned, and managed Ethernet or fiber optic cables. Otherwise, edge data centers need to connect to an external network provider of some kind.

This almost always means fiber optic networks. The provider might be a telecom carrier or a private network service. If the connection point is a cell tower, the network is already there. Other times, it may be necessary to connect the edge data center to the nearest fiber optic network.

Dark Versus Lit Fiber

The United States has been pretty extensively wired up with fiber optic cabling. Certainly, most urban areas have sprawling, overlapping fiber optic networks run by different telecom companies, towercos, and other network operators. Edge data centers are able to connect to these fiber networks, assuming the carrier is willing to make the connection.

This book isn't the right venue to do a deep dive on how fiber works, but briefly, the technology transmits data by means of light pulses that travel through cables made of glass. The nature of the material and the wavelength of light enable fiber to carry massive amounts of data at high speed—far greater bandwidth than what is available with traditional copper cables. Fiber comprises the backbone of the Internet and related telecommunications infrastructure.

Fiber comes in two modes, *dark* or *lit*. Lit fiber has been put into use by the network operator. A building might be *lit* if it has an active fiber optic network connection. In an urban area, it's common to find many lit buildings, especially in a downtown business district. This is also known as a *lit service*.

Dark fiber, in contrast, is fiber optic cabling that has not been put into service by a network carrier. Dark fiber cables are not yet connected to an optical device at either the starting or endpoint point of the fiber run. Carriers install dark fiber with the idea that it will be put to use at some point in the future. It's like an empty building with space ready to rent out.

For an edge data center operator, dark fiber offers a number of advantages over lit fiber. It tends to be less expensive, for one thing. The customer can negotiate for favorable long-term rates.

It is also possible to contract for a dedicated fiber connection with dark fiber. With lit, in comparison, you're sharing the fiber with other customers. You can have virtually unlimited bandwidth with dark fiber. Such exclusive use of fiber translates into stronger security and compliance characteristics for the network. IT teams have complete control over the fiber, too, which has operational and security benefits. Network architects can also design low latency routes, which are helpful in edge computing.

One important factor to note, however, is that dark fiber puts the onus for network uptime on the customer, not the carrier. With a lit or managed service, service delivery, service levels, and equipment maintenance are the responsibility of the carrier. Not so for dark fiber. With dark fiber, you're leasing the infrastructure, so it's up to you to keep it running. There may not be any sort of SLA from the carrier. This can be negotiated, of course. And, there are third-party service providers that can support a network built using dark fiber.

Making the Connection to Fiber

An edge data center needs to connect to fiber, whether it's dark or lit. In the best-case scenario, the chosen location will be right on top of a fiber connection. This might be a lit building or a segment of dark fiber that runs directly underneath or above the data center's location. The goal is to avoid construction to extend the fiber from its trunk line to the data center location.

Extending fiber to a new location is called a *lateral* in the industry. A lateral refers to creating a new fiber network segment from existing fiber infrastructure to the site's minimum point of entry (MPOE) to the existing fiber infrastructure. Sometimes, there will be an existing conduit available to make the connection. Asking for permission to use this conduit, which might be owned by a telco carrier, a cable company or an electric utility, is known as *petitioning*.

Using existing conduit is preferable to digging a trench and laying fiber cable in a construction project. Not only is this costly and time-consuming, the process also requires permits, which add cost, delay, and uncertainty to the project.

The big question, before you even start, is "where is the fiber?" Services like FiberLocator[1] offer detailed interactive maps that show where fiber is located. FiberLocator's maps reveal that fiber can be dense in some areas and sparse in others. There are many reasons for this, including

---

[1] www.fiberlocator.com.

concentration of commercial activity in certain neighborhoods, traditional telephone line paths, and so forth. However, what's important to note is that you cannot assume that fiber is going to be conveniently available where you need it for your edge data center.

Fiber location emerges as a critical element of edge data center site selection. Building long lateral connection to fiber lines can be extremely expensive. If the edge data center's location is non-negotiable, then a high fiber connection cost has to be part of the return-on-investment (ROI) calculation for the site.

If fiber is not an option, which might occur in a rural area, then other modes of connection may suffice. For example, it is possible to connect an edge data center to the Internet using a satellite. A satellite dish can be added to the site, giving the data center a space connection. The speeds may not be as good as fiber, but space offers a lot of flexibility in location.

The *Hairpin* Problem

Discussions about fiber and its role in edge computing need to factor in a potentially serious obstacle to realization of a low latency edge. The problem is the basic design of telecommunications networks. In some telecom networks, packet traffic gets routed through a central office, no matter where the data center is located.

Experts refer to this as a *hairpin* curve. For example, even if a device sends data to a cell tower that's a 100 yards away, the tower might send that data to a central office 10 miles away, and then route it back across the same 10 miles to the edge data center at the base of the tower. Many of the latency advantages of the localized edge data center are lost.

The solution is reengineering telecom networks for edge computing. That is a lot easier said than done, of course. A technology has been developed to correct this problem, but it may take years to deploy. It remains to be seen how serious the hairpin problem will be for edge computing. It's out there, though, and it's wise to be aware of its potential to get in the way of edge plans.

Figure 6.1 Fiber optic cable map

CHAPTER 7

Powering the Edge Data Center

Edge data centers contain a large number of computing devices in a small physical space. The density of this hardware translates into a need for electrical power that's usually a great deal higher than a comparable building that isn't used for this purpose. A 200-square-feet edge data center, for example, might require 100 kW of power for its computers alone. By contrast, a three-bedroom house, which might be 10 times larger, typically needs about 3 kW.[1]

Most of the time, acquiring adequate electrical power for an edge data center is not a major challenge. However, the outsized power needs of an edge site can cause problems in certain cases. The power utility may have to add capacity to existing lines. Municipalities may not want to cooperate, and in this day and age, environmental issues cannot be ignored.

How Much Power Does an Edge Data Center Need?

Estimating power consumption needs for a data center is a complicated process, one that this book will not explore in its full depth. The basic ideas are important to understand, however. One foundational principle to grasp is that an edge data center is essentially a container for a number of electrical appliances. Each of those appliances, whether they are computer servers, network switches, storage arrays, or other devices, uses electricity at a level between a minimum and maximum rate of consumption.

---

[1] "How Much Electricity Should a 3 Bedroom House Use?" n.d. Homex.com.

For example, a server might need between 2,000 and 4,000 watts, depending on what it's doing. A compute intensive workload like artificial intelligence uses more juice than video streaming. And, this power consumption is not proportionate to the device's size. A 1U server of Type A might have triple the power needs of a 1U server of Type B. This is why, colocation companies almost always charge for rack space by the watt, not the U.

Makers of edge data centers describe their products in terms of rack availability and maximum power availability. This can be somewhat confusing, given the potential imbalance between device size and power consumption. A modular micro data center might have room for 10 42U racks, but also a maximum power availability of 100 kW. If a single rack uses up all 100 kW, the other nine racks are going to have to be empty. That's an extreme case, but you get the idea.

Furthermore, that 100 kW is not all the power the data center's needs. That's just for the computer hardware and other IT devices. The data center also has to have electricity to run cooling systems, lights, security systems, and other equipment.

A 100-kW data center might need another 80 kW for cooling and so forth. The overall power need is therefore 180 kW. That's what has to come off the power grid to make the data center operate. The data center industry has come up with a metric to describe the difference between the overall power requirements of a data center and the power it needs to run its computer equipment. This is known as the power usage effectiveness (PUE) ratio.

Right now, the average PUE for a large data center is 1.57.[2] This mean that for every kilowatt used for computing, the data center needs 0.57 kW for cooling and other noncomputing purposes. PUEs have been dropping for years. In 2007, the average PUE was 2.5!

Advances in cooling and improvements and other efficiency gains have driven the numbers down. The RakworX micro data center utilizes a cooling technique that does not involve electricity-powered air conditioning. By adopting the ancient process of water cooling, RakworX can

---

[2] "What Is the Average Annual Power Usage Effectiveness (PUE) for Your Largest Data Center?" n.d. Statista.com.

bring the PUE of its data centers down to 1.1, which is extremely low by industry standards.

Getting PUE down is advantageous for many reasons. For one thing, it saves money. Data center operators want to spend as little as possible on power that isn't going to run revenue-generating servers. In many data center operating agreements, power costs are a pass-through or charged at a slight markup. There's little financial upside to a high PUE. A low PUE is also environmentally friendly, which is becoming an increasingly important issue.

Adding Power to a Site

Connecting the edge data center to the electrical grid is not usually a serious challenge. Most of the time, the process is equivalent to powering up any other built structure. A credentialed electrician does the work, stringing wire from utility poles to a *weatherhead* cap on the data center. The cap protects the wires from water and ice.

In remote locations, it may be necessary to extend the power grid to the data center site. This gets more complicated and expensive. Negotiations with the power utility will determine who pays for it, and what specifications the extension will have to meet.

The main challenges in connecting an edge data center to the power grid arise when there is not enough power available. This can occur for a number of reasons, mostly having to do with location. In a busy downtown area, for example, it may not be possible to bring extra power into an office building. Financial firms run into this problem if they want to have localized compute power for processing financial transactions.

The solution may be to rent more square footage of floor space than the data center actually needs. That way, the data center can draw all the available power for that overall floor space, even if most of it is not utilized. This is not economically efficient, as a firm may have to rent the entire floor of a building in order to run a data center that takes up one-tenth of that floorspace. The financial benefits of localized trading might make it worthwhile, but nonfinancial use cases may make it unworkable. The other option is to generate electrical locally, a once far-fetched idea that is becoming more mainstream with every passing year.

Addressing Limits of Power

Electrical power is not unlimited, and edge computing may put an unbearable strain on the grid in certain areas. The need to concentrate computing in urban areas leads to power demands in places where electricity may not be available.

Mark Thiele, CEO of Edgevana, offered an example of how this problem might play out. "If you want to deploy 50 edge data centers in a 10-block area of a city, each of 100 kW, that's 5 megawatts," he said. "That 10-block area may not have five megawatts to spare. You can't take it from existing buildings."

With larger edge sites, the problem is potentially a lot worse. A 10,000-square-feet edge data center might require five to seven megawatts. "If you deploy 20 of those in a city, which is within the realm of possibilities," Thiele added,

> You're looking at 100 megawatts of extra load, which is about a third of what Las Vegas uses today. The grid simply isn't designed for it, at least not today, and environmental trends do not favor adding so much capacity.

Alternative Energy Sources

The data center industry is embracing alternative energy sources like wind and solar. Data center operators are adopting these alternative methods of electrical generation partly to save money but also for reasons of image and government relations. American data centers use 1.8 percent of all the country's electricity, contributing 0.5 percent U.S. greenhouse gas emissions.[3] That may not sound like a lot, but roughly speaking, data centers use as much electricity as five million people, equivalent to the population of Chicago.

As the public becomes more aware of global warming and the need to reduce carbon emissions, big electricity users like data centers face

---

[3] M. Waters. June 22, 2022. "Energy-Hungry Data Centers Are Quietly Moving Into Cities," *MIT Technology Review*.

pressure to show that they are part of the solution, not the problem. This is about more than public relations, too. Data centers usually need the government to agree to permits for site development and land use. If politicians feel that a data center development is going to make them look like they're not doing enough to promote sustainability, they may not allow the project to proceed.

Edge data centers will face similar pressures. They need permits and zoning variances, so government officials will get to have a say in the data centers' electrical use. For this reason, edge data center operators are looking at solutions like solar panels and wind turbines to provide supplemental power. It's unlikely that an edge data center can function entirely on wind or solar, but these methods can generate a portion of the electricity needed to run the equipment. They can also be part of a battery-based power backup system. In some cases, gas turbines are a solution, though they are not looked upon favorably by environmentalists.

CHAPTER 8

Operating the Edge Data Center

Edge data centers appear somewhat inert from the outside. They're usually metal boxes sitting on concrete pads near cell towers or industrial buildings. Inside, they're almost always devoid of people. Lights on servers and network switches blink in the dark. Yet, there's a lot happening in an edge data center. Reliable operations are critical to whatever mission they're assigned.

Areas of Edge Data Center Operations

An edge data center, whether it's a lone outpost of an IT department or part of a massive edge network, will invariably be the responsibility of a manager or team of some kind. This is an important idea to keep in mind when thinking about what it takes to operate an edge data center. Like any data center, the edge data center is an element of a broader IT and business endeavor. The people and organizational unit responsible for operating the edge data will find themselves focused on critical tasks related to keeping the site running and delivering on its service-level commitments.

Adhering to the Service-Level Agreement (SLA)

An edge data center will almost always be subject to one or more service-level agreements (SLAs). The people who manage it will be bound by an agreement to deliver services at specified levels. The SLA might be an actual legal contract. Other times, the SLA could be an internal agreement inside an organization. Such obligations are no less serious. Violating a contractual SLA can result in a lawsuit. With an internal SLA, a violation could lead to a loss of employment. Each area of edge data center operations should be viewed from the perspective of SLA adherence.

An SLA can cover a variety of services, but in general, it deals with the following areas of operation:

- **Uptime**—IT systems inevitably fail, but IT managers can avoid the most disruptive downtime by implementing redundant capacity and comparable failover techniques. At some point, however, the entire data center will go down. This is impossible to avoid. The cause could be systemic, such as from a cyberattack or software configuration error. It could also be weather related. The question is how long will the outage last? An SLA will often contain a specific metric for uptime, such as 99.99 percent, meaning that an edge data center will not be down more than 52 minutes a year. If the data center is down for two hours, the managing team has violated the SLA.

- **System responsiveness**—The applications and storage devices running in an edge data center may be subject to an SLA that defines how responsive they will be to requests for service. Indeed, such latency metrics are the essence of edge computing. An organization that goes to the trouble and expense of deploying an edge data center may insist on a system response time of one millisecond, for example. If the systems are slower than that, they've violated the SLA. Details matter a lot in this context. For example, the SLA should ideally define the service area where the SLA is in effect. A one millisecond latency may only be possible within a radius of, say, two miles from the site. A service request from farther away should not count for SLA adherence.

- **Support responsiveness and time-to-resolution**—If there is an outage or other incident that affects the edge data center's functioning, the SLA will usually define how quickly the managing entity will respond. For example, an SLA may specify that a request for service in the event of an outage will occur within four hours of it being reported. This sort of requirement is standard in IT. It can be a little tricky in an edge situation, where the data center may be in a remote wilderness area hundreds of miles from the IT department. The requirement will still exist, however, and this is an area of operations where the edge emerges as a distinct challenge in contrast to conventional data centers. How will those responsible take care of the incident quickly enough? Who will do the work? The answers are usually different at the edge. Then, once whoever is responsible has gone into action, how long will it take to resolve the issue? The time-to-resolution may also be covered by the SLA.

Managing the Edge Data Center Technology Stack

Edge data centers, like all data centers, operate what IT professionals call a *technology stack*, depicted in Figure 8.1. Tech stacks vary, of course, but in general, they contain the layers of technology shown in the figure. At the bottom of the stack is the physical facility itself, with the power systems, cooling, security systems, and so forth.

Next up is the network. The data center must connect to a network, such as a corporate network or the Internet. Within the data center itself,

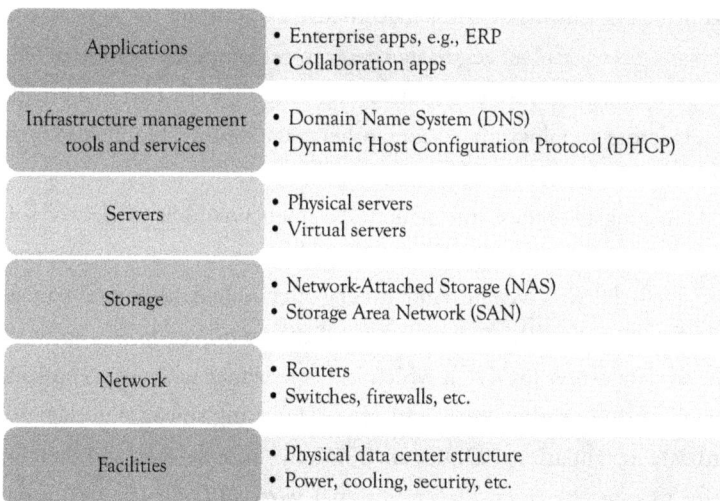

Applications	• Enterprise apps, e.g., ERP • Collaboration apps
Infrastructure management tools and services	• Domain Name System (DNS) • Dynamic Host Configuration Protocol (DHCP)
Servers	• Physical servers • Virtual servers
Storage	• Network-Attached Storage (NAS) • Storage Area Network (SAN)
Network	• Routers • Switches, firewalls, etc.
Facilities	• Physical data center structure • Power, cooling, security, etc.

Figure 8.1 The data center technology stack

hardware devices must be networked together, so routers and switches are present to enable computers to communicate with storage devices and the like.

The storage layer of the technology stack includes devices that store data, as well as the software that enables them to function. Storage in a data center may be configured as *direct-attached storage* (DAS), which means the storage drive (either spinning disk or solid state) is attached to a specific server. Or, storage devices are arranged in a storage area network (SAN) that creates a larger pool of storage than can be available through direct-attached options. Both approaches have their advantages and limitations.

The server layer contains the computing devices that run the data center's software applications. The servers in this layer may be physical machines or virtual machines. However they are configured, the servers are generally the payload of the data center. They're why the data center is there in the first place—to run software that users need.

The top two layers of the tech stack, applications and infrastructure management and tools and services, are completely logical in nature. They are not physical. Rather, these two layers refer to software that runs on the server layer. Application software includes programs like enterprise resource planning (ERP), collaboration platforms, industrial systems management, and the like.

The infrastructure management layer contains software that's needed to run the systems inside the data center. It's important for anyone contemplating the use of an edge data center to get an understanding of what this layer is all about. An edge data center is going to be part of a broader infrastructure topology that spans other data centers, cloud platforms, colocation facilities, and other edge data centers.

Managing all of these infrastructure elements requires specialized software. There is no shortage of excellent solutions for this job. Platforms from Dell, HPE, VMware, and others offer rich data center management functionality. This includes the ability to set up and run a software-defined data center (SDDC), which is a data center wherein computing, storage, and network components are set up using software, rather than hardware instantiation. SDDCs are infinitely more flexible, and therefore useful to edge use cases, than traditional *wires and pliers* modes of data center setup and management.

That said, it's worth noting that edge data centers present a new challenge to existing data center and infrastructure management tools. While in theory, there's no difference between an edge data center and a large-scale core data center, the realities of scale and distance do make edge sites a distinct management challenge.

For example, it can be challenging to manage storage in a data center. Someone, using specialized software, has to stay on top of how much storage is allocated to various virtual servers. If this is hard in a single data center, how would it be to manage storage across a thousand edge data centers? This is where a new class of edge data center management software shows its usefulness.

Emerging edge data center management platforms like NodeWeaver and others are taking on the distinct challenges of managing infrastructure that's spread across numerous edge sites. These platforms are comparable to those used in core data centers, but they employ more automation and purpose-built features that are suited to the sprawl and scale of multiple remote edge sites. NodeWeaver, for example, offers autonomic management of edge assets—self-healing, automatic handling of failovers, adding of storage nodes, and so on.

Physical Hardware Management and Support

At launch, an edge data center is an empty vessel. It contains server racks that need to be filled with hardware to accomplish the site's technology mission. What kind of hardware? Well, like so many matters in this business, the answer, often infuriating, is "It depends."

While data center racks tend to look uniform from the outside, with row after row of servers with black bezels bearing familiar manufacturers' logos, there is actually a breathtaking variety in the design and configuration of server and storage hardware. This book isn't the place to go into depth on this, but it's useful to understand the basic options you have in equipping an edge data center.

The choice may not be yours, of course. In some cases, an edge data center tenant will decide what it wants and procure the necessary hardware. If you're operating the edge site, your job will be to make sure that the available power can support the hardware and then oversee its installation.

If you get to choose the hardware, you will have to consider a number of factors related to performance, purpose, and power consumption. Different workloads favor different types of hardware. For example, AI, data analytics, and other high-performance computing use cases need high-performance computer (HPC) hardware and comparably high-performing storage. This kind of equipment uses more power than equivalently sized standard hardware. With HPC, it's likely that the data center will max out its power before it fills its racks.

Alternatively, certain workloads, like video processing, require very little actual computing. It's a waste of money and energy to run video on a high-performing server. Instead, low-power servers, perhaps those running ARM chips, will be best. However, if you deploy low-power ARM servers to an edge site, you will be limited in your ability to run regular (e.g., Windows or Linux-based) software on those machines.

If your workload is VDI, that will have its own preferred hardware setup. In some cases, VDI actually requires each desktop to have its own dedicated *blade* server. A blade is a small server that sits vertically in a large chassis. A blade system might be 10Us high, the vertical equivalent of 10 standard 1U servers, but it can run 16 blade servers in that space.

If you don't know what your edge site will be running, or if you want the flexibility to change its mission over time, the best approach is probably to outfit it with standard X86 servers. These are exemplified by the Dell PowerEdge and HPE ProLiant lines. There's a lot of variation in processor power, memory, and configurations, but these servers all run Intel or AMD X86 style central processing units (CPUs). They're designed to run the most common Windows Server and Linux operating systems and compatible software.

Installing standard X86 servers with average performance gives you the most flexibility in serving different client needs. It's easy to enable these machines to run VMs and edge cloud architectures. They can be switched easily to other workloads.

Who does the work of installing the equipment? The process of *standing up* servers and storage can be time-consuming. It requires expertise. Many qualified system integrators are available to perform this task.

It may make sense to identify a single firm that can handle the installation, but also the long-term maintenance of the hardware.

An interesting alternative that some edge site operators are taking advantage of involves having the hardware manufacturer preconfigure the hardware. HPE does this, among others. They have a special division that stands up hardware based on client specifications at the factory. They then deliver entire racks of equipment ready to go—they just need to be powered up and connected to the network and they're running. This is a huge time saver and gets you out of the potential problem of having a field technician stuck on an installation issue he or she doesn't understand.

Computer hardware has a lifespan. Opinions vary on this, but the consensus is that a server can operate for about four years before it becomes obsolete. Storage equipment lasts about five years. Some companies compress this lifecycle and try to upgrade their hardware every three years. Others stretch out the hardware lifespan for additional years. At some point, however, the hardware will either fail or become so comparatively slow and energy-hungry that it will make business sense to replace it, even if it still works.

The hardware lifecycle needs to be part of an edge data center's investment model. The data center structure will likely have a far longer potential lifespan than the hardware it hosts. This may or may not be a big issue, but it's something to consider. For instance, a colocation client may want a three-year hosting agreement that matches the lifecycle of their hardware. If they pick up and leave after three years, and the edge data center is empty, that can be a business problem if you're trying to amortize the investment in the edge data center over 10 years. You have a vacancy problem.

Once in operation, hardware support may include processes like reboots and installation of new operating system software. This needs to happen at a distance. The assumption should be that the fewer physical visits to an edge data center, the better. Hardware managers will also be called upon to update device firmware from time to time. Firmware is software embedded in a device's read-only memory (ROM) chip. It is the underlying code that tells the device how to function in its most basic processes, running beneath even the operating system.

Software Management and Support

The edge data center exists to run software. Without software, it's nothing but an expensive structure filled with fancy paperweights. The specific software choice for an edge data center will depend on its purpose. If the site has been set up to run AI, then it will run AI software. If virtual desktops are the reason the edge data center was installed, then it will run VDI, and so forth. Each of these application software programs will run atop an operating system, such as Windows Server or Linux. The site will also be running some collection of system management and data center management software.

Someone, or some team, will have the responsibility of managing and supporting all of this software. Who will do the work will depend on organizational factors for the entity operating the data center. In a large IT department, for example, VDI might have its own system owners. Their entire job is to support VDI. Other times, software management and support will be of a generalized team in IT. Business managers may have a *dotted line* relationship with the people who manage their software.

Whoever the software managers are, their jobs include tasks like updating software, applying security patches, and responding to outages and performance slowdowns. To get this work done, they need remote administration tools that give them the ability to install software and reboot servers. They also need visibility into how the software is performing. If an application slows down or crashes, they need to know as soon as possible.

Network Management and Support

The edge data center is connected to one or more networks. These might be telecom carrier networks, a corporate network, or other privately run networks. The data center also runs its own little internal network, which connects the devices to one another as well as to the external networks. All of these connections must be monitored for slowdowns and outages. The network hardware, such as routers and switches, must be maintained and kept current with regard to its operating software, configurations, and more.

A network manager, or team, is generally responsible for these tasks. The network aspects of an edge data center will likely be monitored and controlled through a network operations center (NOC) room at the entity that runs the site. The NOC room provides network admins with an overview of all network activity in the entire enterprise—along with the ability to respond to problems and alerts.

Maintenance and Support of Power, Cooling, and Physical Plant

The edge data center requires maintenance and support for its dedicated power and cooling systems, as well as its physical plant. In this way, it's no different from a core data center. The difference is that an edge computing entity might be running dozens or even thousands of edge sites, each with its own physical systems.

Someone, or some team, is on point for making sure all of these systems are running as required. This is important work, as an edge data center will not run for very long on battery or backup power, or without cooling. If there is a breach in the physical structure, that can be catastrophic.

Monitoring of physical systems is thus a critical workload. Sensors can alert admins to problems, which they can then resolve either through remote operation of electrical and cooling systems or by dispatching a service firm to the site.

Security

This topic is covered in detail in the next chapter, but briefly, security is another important area of responsibility for the entity that operates an edge data center. This includes both physical and cyber security. A security team, often working in a security operations center (SOC), should be able to monitor the edge data center for threats and incidents that might indicate that a cyberattack is taking place. This team will also be responsible for installing and managing any security-related software, such as endpoint detection and response (EDR) software agents that sit on servers to detect and respond to attacks.

Physical security may be handled by a separate team or service provider. In all likelihood, physical security will be assigned to an external provider that will monitor alarm sensors on the property and video feeds from security cameras. If there is an incident, the company can dispatch its own security people to respond or notify local law enforcement.

Operational Challenges for the Edge Data Center

Running a single, large data center is a major challenge. Doing it right means setting up and managing people and teams with different skills, backgrounds, and mandates, along with associated collections of technology that support the data center's hardware, software, security, and more. Edge data centers represent a different spin on these same challenges. Instead of one giant facility to manage, there will be many. Management processes must adapt to this different set of circumstances.

Modes of Edge Data Center Operations

Three modes of data center operations predominate: Attended, attended/automated mix, and fully automated/unattended. Attended data center operations mean that human admins are present on site to take care of operational needs. If a server has to be replaced or manually rebooted, for example, a person will walk over to the cabinet, unlock it, and perform the task.

Today, almost all data center operational tasks can be performed remotely. They can also be done on an automated basis, meaning that a human admin may not even be aware that a process has occurred. For instance, a server can be configured to install operating system updates and patches automatically.

Or, an admin can issue a command to update operating systems, but the system management software will do the legwork, using automation to install the new OS on thousands of machines. Most large data centers run on an attended/automated mix. People are on site, but automation is doing a lot of the actual data center management work.

A fully automated/unattended data center is one where no people are present, at least not on a full-time basis. This is rare for a major site, but it will almost certainly be the norm for edge data centers. Even if they are close to corporate headquarters, edge sites lack the space for full time staff. And, their numbers would make it unfeasible to staff each edge site even if people and space were available.

Edge data centers will need to run on a fully automated/unattended basis. A physical visit may be necessary at some point, but the assumption is that the site needs to run without anyone there. With that in mind, consider the SLA monitoring and incident response requirements for an edge data center.

Service-Level Monitoring and Incident Response

Someone, or some team (getting to be my new favorite expression), needs to monitor all aspects of the edge data center's functioning to make sure it is meeting its SLA. Who this will be and what software they will use to perform this task are going to vary from one organization to the next. The important thing to get, however, is that someone has to have an overview—clear and immediate knowledge of any issue that affects the SLA, no matter who is responsible for that underlying issue.

This can get complicated pretty quickly. An edge data center might be operated by more than one team, or even by separate companies. Separate groups of people, each with their own software tools and likely reporting up into different areas of the organization, are tasked with hardware, software, network, physical maintenance, and security. Each will have its SLA requirements. All must be connected to whomever's job it is to ensure SLA adherence.

How will this work? Again, it depends. In the best-case scenario, the systems for monitoring and managing hardware, software, and so forth will be integrated with some master data center operations management console. An SLA violation in an operating area like hardware or physical security will instantly send an alert to a data center operations person, who will immediately spring into action to remediate the problem.

A second-best scenario is that the person in charge of each operating area is aware of the SLA and is made personally responsible for correcting any SLA violations on their own. Then, they are supposed to report the incident and what they did about it to whoever owns the edge data center.

This approach avoids software integration, which is costly and potentially time-consuming. But, it relies on more people knowing what's expected of them and taking appropriate actions.

A lot can go wrong. Even in the best case, people have to understand what's expected of them. They need to know the SLA terms and what they mean for the operation. Some management systems can have SLA rules programmed into them. Automated incident response workflows can guide admins in how to react to an SLA violation. However, these setups tend to degrade over time as people come and go, software gets updated, and so forth.

Ultimately, SLA compliance is a people-centric workload. Rules-based and automated systems can help, but without the right human and organizational factors in place, they won't do much. In fact, they can even make things worse. For example, if old SLA rules are not updated, then an SLA violation can come and go without anyone being aware of it. If more than one company is involved in managing the edge data center and adhering to the SLA, the organizational aspects of the workload are even more potentially unmanageable.

Lights-Out Management (LOM)

Getting an edge data center to operate in adherence to its SLAs, but do so on an unattended/fully automated basis means embracing a mode of data center administration known as lights-out management (LOM). LOM involves remotely managing systems *out-of-band*, that is, when a system is not online. LOM system enables data center admins to manage the infrastructure as if they were in the same physical space, but in reality, the admins can be anywhere.

Tasks that can be performed with the right LOM solutions up and running include starting a system, even if it has been powered down. They can stop a system from running, reboot it, restart a fan, or affect other physical hardware components. LOM enables admins to monitor system health and view system logs from afar.

An LOM system usually has a hardware element present in the data center. This might be called the *LOM Module*. If the LOM Module is part of the hardware itself, a common manufacturer offering, it may be called integrated lights-out management or ILOM. Data center admins can access the LOM Module through a remote console.

Dell calls their ILOM product *Integrated Dell Remote Access Controller*. It's available with PowerEdge servers. Cisco has its Integrated Management Controller (IMC). These tools are sometimes called *baseboard management controllers* or BMCs. LOM systems also need a connection to the network, a communication protocol, and software.

Uptime Institute Data Center Tiers and the Edge

The Uptime Institute is the authoritative organization setting standards for reliability in the data center industry. If you are considering deploying an edge data center, you will likely encounter them or someone who wants their guidance in the process. Data center professionals have been working with Uptime's data center tiers and standards for many years. If you're new to this, here is a brief overview that may help you understand what they're talking about.

The Uptime Institute has established a system for rating data centers for the ability to delivery uptime, or continuous operations. The tiers are based on objective standards and a certification process. The certification comes from an audit of the data center's design, equipment, and operating procedures, among other factors.

- A data center with a Tier I classification is considered to have a basic capacity, for example, for an office. It will include an uninterruptible power supply (UPS), an area for IT systems, dedicated cooling that runs outside of business hours, and an engine generator in case of power outages. A Tier I data center protects systems from human errors, but it is not expected to handle system failures or outages. It will have to shut down for maintenance.
- A Tier II data center has redundant capacity for power and cooling, including chillers and cooling units, heat rejection equipment, and fuel tanks. It enables greater uptime and reliability, a *critical environment*, in the Uptime Institute's words. Its design enables the data center to operate while

components of it are being maintained. However, as with a
Tier I facility, a Tier II facility can experience and outage in
the event of an unexpected shutdown.

- A Tier III data center is concurrently maintainable. Its main
differentiator from a Tier II facility is a set of redundant
components and redundant distribution paths. It does not
require a shutdown for maintenance.

- A Tier IV data center is characterized by having multiple
independent and physically isolated systems. These function
as redundant capacity components and distribution paths.
The separation prevents an event in one area from affecting
other systems.

As you might imagine, as you go up the tiers, the more expensive
the data center is to build and run. The major hyperscale facilities are at
Tiers III and IV. Their business cases justify the higher investment and
operating costs.

So, at what tier would an edge data center find itself? Good
question... The simple answer is *none*. The best equipped edge data
centers might pass a Tier I audit. The Uptime Institute, aware of the
growth of edge data centers, has started its *TIER-Ready* design review
program to help edge data center customers get the reliability they need
from edge facilities. As of now, several makers of modular data center
equipment are certified as TIER-Ready partners.

Making Edge Data Center Operations Affordable

If all of this seems like a lot to manage on a budget, it is. The economical
operation of multiple edge sites presents a major challenge. Organizations
that want to deploy dozens or possibly hundreds or thousands of edge
data centers will likely need to develop new approaches to data center
operations if they want to control costs.

It will not work to apply existing organizational and technological
modes of data center management, which were designed for a small
handful of big facilities, to the edge. The costs will be too high, even if it
is possible to find all the people who would be required for such a setup.

Instead, edge data center owners need to think differently about every aspect of data center operations.

What this will actually look like remains to be seen. However, a few general directions and new assumptions are already evident. The most basic assumption is that there needs to be a new generation of data center management software designed specifically for the edge. This may turn out to be an evolution of existing infrastructure management tools, but it could also be a wholly new system.

The updated tooling would have to streamline processes of monitoring, alerting, and follow up for any sort of incident that affects edge data center uptime. Incident response workflows would have to be highly automated, minimizing people's time spent initiating tasks like reboots, alarm checks, and the like. Economy of human effort should be the guiding principle of these new tools.

Mark Thiele, CEO of Edgevana, offered a perspective. He said:

> If I can put, a thousand locations out at the edge, and send one person out to work on all of them, or five people instead of one for every five locations or something—that's a huge benefit to me. But I can only do that if I have a lot of automation around how I can manipulate the hardware in the location. And that's not just the hardware, but it's the environmental security, the software. It's kind of like being able to manage a satellite that's, you know, a million miles from Earth, you need to be able to do almost everything, including rewrite the code to get the thing to keep working, right.

It is partly architectural, according to Thiele. For automated site management to be effective, the workloads cannot be dependent on a particular site or hardware. When this is the case, admins can switch out servers and disk drives without concern about the workload. Alternatively, if the workload is dependent on specific equipment, then maintenance and incident response will require people to take action, often physically, with trucks and scheduling. This is highly inefficient.

Organizationally, it will probably make sense to create converged teams or roles to stay on top of edge sites. It is impractical and prohibitively expensive for separate teams for software support, hardware, security, networks, and physical systems to work in a matrix across N number of edge sites. Rather, a better approach would be to converge responsibility for software, hardware, and so forth into a single team or role. With the right software tools, this new single team or person could have a complete overview of all relevant systems and be able to initiate and track responses to problems as they arise in any one area.

The cost accounting side of the equation also deserves attention. This is an underappreciated area for data center operators. It hasn't been a big issue because allocating costs across three or four big facilities is not too difficult. With N number of sites, new accounting software has to be able to track expenses on a site-by-site basis.

Outsourcing of services will likely become more prevalent and important at the edge than it is at the core. Managed services may make sense when an edge data center owner starts to look at the costs and difficulties in recruiting and retaining the personnel needed for 24/7/365 site management. Indeed, a new class of outsourced data center management services will probably emerge from the move to edge computing. These companies already exist, but they may find it advantageous to expand their offerings to take a bigger role in managing edge sites.

CHAPTER 9

Securing the Edge Data Center

Edge data centers are challenging for security practitioners, as they tend to turn most established security policies on their heads. For example, instead of having to operate a single *man trap* at a large facility, edge security managers need to track dozens, or possibly hundreds of man traps at self-contained sites. The physical attack surface area at the edge is far larger than at the core. Innovative countermeasures and best practices are emerging, however, that enable a robust security posture at the edge.

Risk Exposure in the Edge Data Center

Understanding cybersecurity challenges and making security plans always starts with an assessment of risk, threats, and vulnerabilities. To keep things simple, we will use the basic information security (InfoSec) *CIA Triad* of confidentiality, integrity, and availability to define risks at the edge. Anything that can affect the confidentiality, integrity, or availability of data or systems at the edge should be considered a threat. The edge faces similar threats to those affecting core facilities. The levels of risk exposure, however—the probability that a threat or vulnerability will result in an actual attack—are different at the edge.

- Physical threats—including everything from weather or other natural disasters (e.g., earthquakes, wildfires) to accidents or malicious human behavior like vandalism. A physical threat might also mean an intruder breaking into an edge site with a specific purpose in mind, like stealing a storage device.

- Cyber threats—covering the full gamut of network-borne attacks, from ransomware to worms, denial-of-service (DoS) attacks, data exfiltration malware, and beyond.
- Human threats—ranging from insider attacks to fraud and spear phishing.

How Security at the Edge Differs From Security at the Core

The edge does not present many novel security challenges, but it does distort the levels of risk for well-known threats. For example, in a hyperscale data center, the risk of an unauthorized individual accessing physical devices is relatively low. In an edge data center, that risk is far higher.

According to Christopher Prewitt, CTO at Inversion6, a managed security service provider (MSSP), the main security challenge at the edge is architectural in nature. As he explained, while it is already somewhat challenging to develop a clear understanding of where one's data and other digital assets are located in a core facility, at the edge, this task becomes exponentially more difficult. "Where are these things going to live and who has access?" he asked.

He elaborated, saying:

It's one thing for a CDN to have public data that they're serving up all across the globe. It's another to have sensitive data now being either served up or updated all across the globe, and in a distributed environment. This data may be getting updated in some central repository somewhere, but it needs to be synced and updated across applications at all edge location. This setup creates a lot of risk exposure. All of this needs to be thought out.

A multiplicity of locations compounds the routine process of data updating, to name one of many IT workloads that get riskier at the edge. He asked:

How do we know that an application is alive at the edge? You have to update its data. It's another layer of complexity, another layer of authentication and authorization that need to occur. You have to think through all the layers of your architecture, understand your machine-to-machine permissions, as well as your human user permissions.

It could be even more complicated, as Prewitt sees things. He added, "Parts of the architecture could be micro services, so your application is leaving your web server and going into what is essentially someone else's web server that's living at the edge."

For Prewitt, the edge creates another tier in the standard three-tier application stack.

On top of your traditional web server, application server and database server tier, you've got a data access tier. That's four tiers, but the edge is really a fifth tier. Each tier makes things harder to manage and secure, especially when that fifth tier is distributed across dozens of edge sites.

Given this architectural complexity, which amplifies risk exposure, system owners and security managers must grapple with user experience, system performance, and access controls. "Without compromising on end user experience, which relates to latency, you have to make sure that only authorized and authenticated users are accessing the applications at the edge," he said.

Physical security is another major area of concern at the edge. Edge data centers may be deployed in high population areas where thousands of people will see them. A person intent on vandalizing the site or stealing its contents will be able to get within a few feet of it, perhaps even right up to the door. A truck could smash into it, too. Of course, most edge data center designs feature robust physical security, but the unfortunate fact is that these sites are exposed in ways that a traditional core data center never will be.

Thinking About Different Countermeasures for the Edge

Best practices and standard security policies for securing edge data centers are emerging in the industry. Some policies are new, such as requiring motion detection sensors on hard drives to detect if the unit has been stolen. The edge also makes optional controls, like hardening servers against physical access, mandatory at the edge. Frequent, automated hardware inventorying is also a good idea.

With heightened physical access risks in mind, standard security practices like identity and access management (IAM) and privileged access management (PAM) need to become more rigorous. For instance, if a malicious actor can establish an administrative account for himself, he may be able to enter an edge site and modify server settings or exfiltrate data before being detected.

For Prewitt, the solution is to use business value to drive decisions about where to focus security resources. "The edge really pushes the old idea that you can't defend everywhere," he said. "Because now, you are everywhere, so you have to concentrate on what's critical." He recommends developing a heat map of digital asset criticality to guide decisions about where to deploy the most rigorous, resource-intensive countermeasures.

With that in mind, data security at the edge starts to look different from the way it does at the core. The risk of data loss is higher at the edge, due to risks of theft, vandalism, and physical interference with the server. For this reason, edge data centers should be configured with frequent backups. Data also needs to be encrypted at the edge, in case someone is able to access the device without authorization.

As these policies and practices coalesce, it may be optimal to think of the entire edge data center as an endpoint. Like an endpoint, it is outside the core of the network. It is at greater risk for attacks, both physical and logical, than core digital assets. Endpoint detection and response (EDR) solutions may need to be adapted to cover entire micro data centers, rather than just specific machines.

Incident response workflows should similarly adapt to handle attacks on edge data centers. The changes to workflows may be subtle, but it is worth reviewing current playbooks to look for areas where having many distributed data centers is a factor, versus responding to incidents in a single core data center. The notifications and procedures will likely need to be different.

Security has to evolve if organizations want to defend digital assets hosted in edge data centers. The edge does not represent a radical shift in

IT, but edge data centers are different enough that security managers need to rethink their countermeasures. In particular, they should recalibrate the emphasis they place on physical risks, as well on how heightened physical security risks affect standard policies for data security and access control.

Understanding Areas of Responsibility for Security

Who will be responsible for all of these new and different edge security policies and practices? The simplest, probably best answer is that the existing security team should shoulder the burden. However, they will need an updated toolset and mindset.

The current best practice is to establish a security operations center (SOC) to act as the organized core of security policy definition, enforcement, and incident response. The SOC is the nexus of security activity. It's where monitoring systems terminate, providing security analysts with alerts and data they can parse to determine if a threat is active, or an attack is underway.

Today, the SOC provides security analysts with a view of security activity affecting on-premises infrastructure, colocated digital assets, cloud-hosted assets, and network endpoints. Depending on the organization, a separate network operations center (NOC) tracks network activity and network security activities. Or, the SOC handles network security, while the NOC deals with network management.

As an organization expands at the edge, it needs to add edge infrastructure to its SOC apparatus. What this will look like remains to be seen. However, initially, what's likely to happen will be edge data center sites being added to SOCs as if they were simply more colocation facilities. This approach will work, up to a point. As the scale of edge deployments grows, however, it becomes untenable. Handling a thousand edge sites as if they were a thousand colocation sites will be overwhelming.

Instead, what needs to happen is the development of edge-specific security monitoring and management tools that can plug into existing SOCs. (This is my free tip to enterprising product managers in the SOC software business.) These tools would almost certainly be powered by artificial intelligence and automation. They would be able to ingest and parse a huge volume of security event data from all edge sites in real time—flagging suspicious activity and issuing alerts to security analysts.

As edge security alerts come up, the SOC team needs an effective way of responding to them. This is a big challenge in security right now, but it will only get more difficult with large edge deployments. Today, some SOCs rely on security orchestration, automation, and response (SOAR) solutions to handle the high-stakes, fast-paced process of security incident response. SOAR automates processes like implementing threat response *playbooks*, sending notification e-mails, and opening IT support tickets.

SOAR will have to adapt to the edge, as well, connecting its automated response workflows with people on the ground wherever the edge sites are located. This is an evolution in SOAR capabilities, not a radical change. For example, using SOAR right now to notify local law enforcement agencies as part of incident response workflows is relatively rare. However, if an organization has a thousand edge sites in small towns, each standing in physical isolation, being able to alert the local police if there's a physical attack will probably be an essential SOAR capability.

Edge security will also involve more external entities than are typically employed in enterprise security today. While outsourcing to MSSPs is becoming increasingly common, with the edge, MSSPs and comparable service providers will most likely provide the majority of the security support. This is because the edge will be everywhere the central organization is not. Unless the organization wants to employ a large team of remote security people—a virtual impossibility today—then they are going to rely on outside service providers.

Doing edge security right will mean thinking differently about most security processes. It means thinking about large numbers of external, detached sites versus a small number of owned or rented platforms. Revamping the security mindset for the edge may be a challenge for some teams, but as tooling develops, the mindset will likely follow.

One final note here about SASE, the secure access service edge. SASE is becoming the standard model for securing end users, endpoint devices, and data as people and digital assets migrate away from centrally defended environments. Though SASE includes the word *edge*, that refers to a logical, not necessarily physical edge. SASE may or may not mean the deployment of actual edge data centers. It is possible to have SASE without any edge infrastructure at all.

CHAPTER 10

Selecting Sites for the Edge Data Center

Location is edge computing's raison d'être. The edge is about deploying computing and data storage to locations where they can deliver low latency system performance or fast, localized data management. Determining the right location is therefore critical to success with the edge.

Deploying an edge data center involves two distinct challenges. First is to find the right location. The second is to determine if an edge data center can, in fact, be deployed at that location. In urban environments, this can be a problematic proposition.

Workload-Driven Parameters for an Edge Data Center Site

Where should an edge data center go? According to Mark Thiele, the data center's workload should be the main guiding factor in selecting a location. A workload needs to have a reason to be at the edge. Otherwise, it would be more convenient and economical to host it at an existing core facility. The workload might require latency for users in a specific geographic area, for example. It might require proximity to datasets coming from a factory floor.

Location might be dictated by proximity to cloud resources. This could be the case in IoT or industrial data management workloads where it makes sense to have cloud computing nearby that can perform data analytics. Or, a cloud provider wants to put computing near where their customers are located. This is happening, for example, with the AWS-Verizon joint edge service offering.

A cluster of enterprise users could also drive site selection for an edge data center. There might be a dozen large enterprises situated within a few miles of one another outside a major city, for instance. If there is no existing cloud or hyperscale colocation data center nearby, it might make sense to deploy an edge data center to provide low latency application services or localized data processing.

A variant of this last example involves large enterprise technology providers deploying instances of their cloud platforms or SaaS products near major clients. To take a hypothetical example, Oracle Cloud might decide it's optimal to create an instance of the platform next to an industrial site in a rural area. This decision makes the platform far more responsive to users at the industrial site and saves a great deal of money on bandwidth.

Data sovereignty regulations could be a factor as well. This is a serious issue in Europe, where EU regulations place strict constraints on the storage and movement of data about EU citizens. An ecommerce business operating in the EU might need to set up edge data center sites in each of the EU's 27 countries to avoid storing a French citizen's personal identifiable information (PII) in Germany, for example. Doing so would put them at risk for a fine.

Data-based restrictions on SaaS deployment can also lead to edge site development. Certain countries do not allow citizens' data to be stored on Salesforce.com, for example, if the app is hosted in another country. However, there might still be users in those countries who want access to the SaaS app. A solution is to set up an edge data center that can access the SaaS app from a nearby country, while keeping citizens' data segregated.

In the United States, this is less of a problem, though laws are changing here as well, especially with regard to privacy. A business might want to separate PII from California residents from PII of customers from other states because of strictures imposed by the California Consumer Privacy Act (CCPA). That could drive the decision to set up an edge data center.

New workloads like metaverses and blockchain similarly exert a gravitational pull on edge data center locations. Metaverse and gaming workloads demand low latency. While they may seem trivial to a corporate computing professional, they are in fact major businesses with millions of paying customers. Companies like Meta have the resources to build or patronize significant edge networks if they so choose.

Owners of blockchain workloads may elect to deploy at the edge for reasons of cost. Moving data centers to rural areas, for instance, may enable a blockchain operator to take advantage of inexpensive land and low-cost electricity. This tactic is proving to be controversial, with rural communities regretting that they welcomed the construction of blockchain/cryptocurrency data center sites. In some cases, these sites make too much noise, create fire hazards, and drive up electricity prices.

Sustainability is also a factor affecting edge data center site selection. This may be news to some, given the criticism that edge computing has received over its energy use. The reason edge computing is environmentally friendly has to do with the surprisingly high amounts of electricity required to power networks. Moving data large distances is neither free nor energy-neutral.

According to Mark Thiele, as much as 40 percent of the electrical load for IT infrastructure is consumed by the network. Shortening network distances and reducing use of bandwidth cut down on electrical consumption. Keeping data close to where it's born is a green strategy.

Edge computing may thus become an element of a corporation's overall environmental, social, and governance (ESG) strategy. ESG is a framework that purports to increase an enterprise's value by incorporating the assessment and management of sustainability-related risks and opportunities into its business operations and strategic planning.

Site Selection Process

With workload-driven parameters in mind, the question then becomes where exactly can this edge data center go? The first step in answering this question involves identifying the best geographic area for the site. Workload and use case will again affect location requirements. For example, data storage required for data sovereignty might fit into a large geographic area, for example, "Somewhere in Berlin." By contrast, an autonomous vehicle use case might easily require an edge data deployed within a radius of a quarter mile of a specific set of map coordinates.

The location radius must then run the gauntlet of strictures affecting edge data center deployment: Is there enough electricity? Will the zoning permit the site to exist? Is there fiber available? And, of course, is there a property available for the use? The tighter the geographic radius, and the denser the urban environment, the more difficult the site selection process can become.

The best approach is often to figure out what's already there. You might be surprised how many small-to-medium scale data centers have already been built in major urban areas. Many of these are private, perhaps owned by local banks, but some are available for rent. Other times, it might be a wise move to buy a local bank's data center. Who knows? They might be eager to offload it. Stranger things have happened. A bank that built a data center in the 1980s could now view it as a financial albatross—but for you, it's a life saver.

Mark Thiele found a solution for an edge computing client with a utility company that had installed dozens of equipment management cabinets throughout a major city. For a purpose wholly unrelated to IT or edge computing, the utility owned phonebooth-sized units with *power, ping, and pipe*. He is in negotiations with the utility to sublet space in these units for edge computing purposes. Each cabinet will become an edge data center.

Experience is showing that zoning can be the biggest obstacle to edge data centers. Michael Siteman had been contracted to deploy a modular edge data center as a backup site for a cloud computing company. The location had to be within a specific area of a city in Southern California.

He found a site that met all of their criteria. It was in the right place. It was convenient to fiber. In fact, no fewer than eight telecom carriers had fiber available to the site. It had a full megawatt of available electricity. And, it was a vacant lot, a rarity in this relatively dense urban area. The owner of the lot was more than happy to lease the space to this mechanical tenant. (Landlords love the idea of renting space to computers. They won't complain that their drains are clogged, and so forth.)

Then, they started talking to the city. All they wanted to do was pave the lot, put in a fence and a concrete pad, and install a modular micro data center. The answer was a firm, irreversible "No way." The block was not zoned for this use, and the city was not going to make an exception. No permit was forthcoming. So, despite all of the great characteristics of the site and the availability of a deal, the location was scrapped.

Siteman then had to go searching nearby for another location. This became a three-bears scenario, where each building and lot they inspected was not quite right. The sites were too small, too expensive, too fiber-deprived, and on and on. Eventually, they found an industrial property that would lease them enough space for the micro data center pod.

This frustrating experience shows how challenging it can be to find a site for an edge data center. What's particularly notable here is that the city in question is known for being quite business-friendly. It's an industrial city. Why they were so adamantly opposed to an edge data center is not clear.

What is clear, however, is that zoning laws are going to have to change if edge computing is going to grow the way most analysts expect it to. At some point, municipalities will probably realize that their citizens value technology performance more than aesthetics or land-use restrictions. They will likely loosen constraints on data centers at that point.

The Great Inversion: How the Edge Upends Traditional Digital Real Estate

The site selection and acquisition process for edge data centers is not occurring in a vacuum. There is already a mature digital real estate business that theoretically serves the needs of edge computing companies. The problem is that edge computing often presents challenges that digital real estate firms are not set up to handle.

The traditional digital real estate business is driven by considerations of cost, scale, and control. In general, the winning strategy has been to build the largest possible facilities at the lowest possible cost. This is why the major data center REITs build and operate hyperscale facilities outside of metropolitan areas.

There is absolutely nothing wrong with this model, and it is likely to endure over the long term. It's just not suited to the edge. Edge computing is driven almost entirely by considerations of latency. Cost, scale, and control are secondary factors in the development and location of edge data centers.

To achieve ultra-low latency across a service area, it is necessary to place compute capacity in locations that are reliably close to the devices that need this kind of fast response. The problem is that the very concentration of user devices that creates the need for ultra-low latency occurs in populated areas—places that are already saturated with developed real estate.

Thus, the edge requires the acquisition of a large number of small, expensive properties. This is the opposite of what digital real estate companies have dealt with, or what they want to do. Today's digital real estate business is defined by relationships, manual processes, and one-off deals. This has worked well for hyperscalers, but it won't meet the anticipated needs of edge computing companies.

Imagine that a company wants to deploy edge computing capacity at the rate of one micro data center per square mile in a city. That would mean that Los Angeles, for example, would need 500 edge sites. This may seem like a high number, but the advent of 5G, with its high antenna density, makes such an estimate realistic, or even low when you consider mobile device growth rates.

If you asked a commercial real estate broker in the digital category to find 500 locations to buy or lease for the purposes of an edge center in Los Angeles—and that each location needed to be close to fiber optic cable—this individual would probably hang up the phone and block your number.

A digital real estate broker earns commission on gross deal value, and the earning potential for brokering a deal for a 1,500-square-foot micro data center site would be on the small side for such a person. To earn a small commission, the broker would have to comb through commercial real estate listings and manually identify properties that have adequate electrical power and fiber connectivity. The owners of these properties would have to agree to lease space to a new class of tenant. The incentive for the broker simply isn't there.

Can this problem be solved? The good news is that, in certain cases, it will solve itself. A telecom company could deploy edge data centers to its existing cell tower and switch locations. This may be easier said than done in some urban environments, though Verizon recently started deploying 5G antennas in old phone booth locations in New York City. It is possible, especially if the telco already has some rights to the sites, as the New York example suggests. It may also be possible for edge computing companies to partner with retail chains that already have many available locations.

Otherwise, solving the edge real estate challenge will require some innovation and new ways of thinking about digital real estate. Automation of the property search and qualifying processes will be critical to success. It will also be necessary to engage with property owners and educate them about the business value of edge site leasing.

Going further, success in edge real estate will involve rethinking assumptions about control over facilities. In the Los Angeles example, it is unlikely that any one entity will own and control all 500 sites. Subleasing of capacity between site owners will become a fact of life for edge computing companies. The process for identifying edge capacity subleasing will also have to be automated. This involves multiedge technologies, a topic I will explore in Chapter 12.

Financing Edge Data Centers

One of the most important and least addressed questions that arises in discussion about the future of edge computing is, "Who is going to pay for all of this?" It's all well and good for me and others to say that the United States will be home to tens of thousands of edge data centers. These data centers will cost money, and it's not at all clear where that money will come from. This reality presents both an obstacle to the realization of edge computing strategies but also a significant opportunity.

The edge is currently in a classic chicken versus egg moment, the kind that has bedeviled other new technology trends going back over 40 years. The technology is available. Customers will not buy it until there is a clear business case for doing so. (And why would they act any other way?) That business case is not entirely evident. Or, at a minimum, it's not proving itself financially.

This issue arose in a recent conversation I had with a principal at company that owns and operates 300 cell towers. He said his company was interested in going into the edge computing business, but so far, they had not seen strong enough client interest. And, clients would not be serious until the cell tower company had edge data center capacity to lease. Chicken, meet egg.

If this cell tower company wants to deploy an edge data center to the base of each of its towers, what sort of investment are we talking about? It depends. (I know you hate it when I use that phrase, but it's applicable.) For the sake of argument, let's assume that a 10-rack edge data center pod costs U.S.$1 million to purchase and deploy. Add in some working capital and new hiring and you're looking at an outlay of about U.S.$400 million for this company to get into the edge computing business.

That's a big bite. Even if this company had that sort of money—and they don't—no serious business executive would authorize an investment of that size without a bulletproof business case. Such a business case does not yet exist. I can make a good argument that the business case is coming soon, but that won't wash. So, this cell tower company, like many others in the almost-edge category, is waiting for the right business conditions to arrive.

Here is also where cultural difference between real estate firms and tech firms become pronounced. Towercos are in the real estate business. They thrive by being conservative with investments. That's not how tech works. Tech firms require big, highly speculative investments with big upsides. The lack of forward motion springs partly from this misalignment of strategies.

Will anyone break this logjam? Someone will, and it will probably involve companies making bold bets and, if history is any guide, some massive mistakes that unintentionally benefit others. Some investor will decide that it's time to shell out U.S.$400 million to deploy 300 edge data centers—a *build it and they will come* strategy. They may not come, and those 300 data centers will be auctioned off for a fraction of what they cost to build. Bad news for the investor, but good news for everyone else.

Alternatively, the large CapEx of edge computing creates an opportunity for financial intermediaries. The towerco in our example is rightly balking at making a U.S.$400 million capital investment in edge data centers. However, if a financing company could put up the money, and lease the edge data centers to the towerco, the deal might look attractive.

That doesn't solve the *and they will come* problem, but the principle of the deal still stands. Another approach would be for a business, such as a colocation provider, to partner with the towerco to finance the data centers. The colo company has the tenants for those edge data centers. The towerco has the mobile connectivity and the real estate. There's a partnership to be formed here. What's important to understand is that without the towerco's land, towers, and fiber connections, it would cost the colo company closer to a billion dollars to get into the edge business.

I suspect that this latter type of partnership will be how the eggs at the edge, so to speak, will hatch. Mutually beneficial alliances that serve to reduce CapEx and risk will create opportunities to invest in edge data center capacity.

CHAPTER 11

Novel Edge Data Center Locations and Form Factors

Computers inevitably follow human activity, wherever that may be occurring. Examples include outer space and military operating environments. As use cases evolve, stakeholders may see advantages to deploying data centers to a range of novel locations. Such may also translate into new form factors that challenge our understanding of what constitutes a data center.

Edge Data Centers in Space

Space exploration and the development of the modern computer are inextricably linked. This history has mostly been forgotten, but it was the Apollo moon missions of the 1960s that catalyzed the creation of solid-state computer circuitry and miniaturization. The Apollo lunar module and command modules both needed onboard computers, and the existing computers of the day were way too large and heavy for the job.

Similarly, space travel and space-based espionage drove the standardization and development of what we now call digital imaging. Satellites and spacecraft had to transmit photos back to earth. Standards bodies came up with digital image formats that could be transmitted by radios from space to ground station.

The relationship between computing and space continues today. The current challenges are manifold. For example, there is a big differential in development time between a space mission and computing device. It might take 10 years to design and build a satellite, including its computer components. By the time the satellite launches, the computer is out of date.

For example, the International Space Station (ISS) uses computers running Intel 80286SX CPUs dating back to the 1980s. This results in several problems, including suboptimal performance and costly and cumbersome support. Having engineers on earth update a 20-year-old computer system that no one remembers building is not ideal.

There is also the problem of data transmission from space. Data has to travel from space to earth using microwaves. This comes with bandwidth constraints. In many cases, it is preferable to process the data where it originates. Deploying computers into space for this purpose makes a lot of sense. The challenge is to do it in a way that's relatively easy to manage.

This is where the space-based edge data center comes into play. Currently in its infancy, the concept of the edge data center in space is being actively pursued by companies like HPE. Their HPE Spaceborne Computer-2, comprising a set of HPE Edgeline Converged EL 4000 Edge and HPE ProLiant servers, was deployed to the ISS in 2021.[1]

The idea is to provide sufficient computing power to the space location. This avoids the necessity for moving data back to earth for processing. Spaceborne Computer-2 is specifically configured for data analytics. It can run all sorts of analysis on data gathered by the ISS.

The other advantage of Spaceborne Computer-2, at least in theory, is that it can be managed remotely as if it were any other data center. System administrators on earth can install software patches, update operating systems, and so forth. The unit's standardized 19-inch rack enables ISS crews to install new hardware with relative ease. Of course, that hardware has to arrive by rocket, but the principle still stands. With Spaceborne Computer-2, the ISS can enjoy up-to-date computing infrastructure.

The project has run into some interesting and unexpected challenges. For instance, solid-state drives (SSDs), which are basically large-scale thumb drives used for data storage, tend to fail in space. They are sensitive to the radiation and magnetic fields in space, which are far stronger than they are on earth.

There is a great deal of rich innovation going on right now in space-based data center development. Solutions are in the works for ever more

---

[1] M. Korolov. January 18, 2022. "Space Is the Final Frontier for Data Centers," Data Center Knowledge.

powerful and efficient data center systems for satellites and deep space probes. Most of the work in this field is concentrating on image processing for satellites, but numerous space-based computing workloads are being studied for their applicability for edge data centers in space.

Military Edge Data Centers

The use of computers in military operations is not a new phenomenon. Indeed, some of the first computers ever built were created to calibrate artillery pieces, crack enemy codes, and figure out how to turn uranium into a weapon. Today, however, military computing use cases have grown fantastically sophisticated and data-intensive. This requires a new approach to computing and storage infrastructure, or at least a thorough analysis of the issue.

Setting aside routine military workloads like payroll and logistics, which can be handled by traditional infrastructure, a variety of evolving military workloads do argue for pushing computing and storage to the edge. These include the storage of data in intelligence collection, the use of data analytics in the field, and the employment of AI in intelligence and weapons operations. Each of these use cases favors having significant data storage capacity and deep computing capabilities as close to combat as possible.

The modern military generates, ingests, and analyzes immense volumes of data. Data sources include a host of satellite systems, radar, electromagnetic spectrum-sensing devices, and more. Starting around the year 2000, the U.S. military adopted a framework known as network-centric operations. Net-centric warfare, as the technology became known, involved creating interconnected networks for gathering, storing, and distributing data based on a service-oriented architecture (SOA).

Net-centric warfare was effective at improving military operations because users of military data, such as commanders in the field and cen-tral command staffs, could all see and use the same data pretty much in real time. The process reduced many (but not all) of the data siloes that had hamstrung military operations in the past.

The military has run into the same *data gravity* problem as industry, however. Net-centric warfare requires moving large amounts of data across global networks and storing it in centralized data repositories. There are two problems with this approach. One is that it is time-consuming to move data across networks. *Real time* becomes delayed time, and in a combat situation, that can be deadly.

To understand the seriousness of this issue, consider that AI is becoming more integrated into the operations of weapons systems. As of today, a human being must still make the decision to fire a weapon, but increasingly, the decision-making process is left up to AI-based software. This makes sense if one thinks about how the decision to fire a weapon today may involve the simultaneous analysis of hundreds of data streams: from satellites, troop position sensors, radar, radio intercepts, and so forth. AI can sort it out more quickly and accurately than a human brain and make a recommendation—fire, or don't fire.

AI in weapons only works if the data is fresh, however. If the AI support system for a missile, say, knows that the enemy was in a position 10 minutes ago, but not where the enemy is now, it will make a fire/don't fire recommendation that could lead to a missile hitting empty space. In fact, the missile could even become *friendly fire* that kills the wrong troops.

The other issue is data security. Networks can be tapped. Encryption is an effective countermeasure, up to a point, but everyone understands that if victory or defeat is at stake, the enemy will spare few efforts or expenses to crack that encryption.

To speed up access to data and reduce the attack surface area, it makes sense to deploy edge data centers closer to areas of military operations. The net-centric model still holds. The data is just closer at hand.

This is currently happening, though it's early in the technology lifecycle. Defense contractors are building portable data centers that can be towed or parachuted into position at forward operating bases (FOBs). All relevant sensor and intelligence data is stored and process locally at the FOB. Commanders have essentially instant access to it, so their analysis and resulting decisions will be based on more accurate information.

In some cases, the weapons platform itself has so much on-boarding computing capacity that it can work as a data center if necessary. The details of this are classified, but the general understanding is that weapons like the F-35 can be configured to create data center functionality in clusters. For instance, if four F-35s are in flight together, they can collectively store and process combat operations data just as a centralized data center would. Navy ships, for sure, already have large-scale data storage and processing capabilities built in, though it's not known how much they are used as edge data centers.

Deploying edge data centers to forward areas solves the latency and data gravity problems facing the military. It also solves some, but not all, of the security risks. One could argue, successfully, that having intelligence and combat operations data stored in FOBs puts the military at greater risk than storing it in a hyperscale facility in Virginia. An FOB can be attacked, and its edge data center could be captured by the enemy. (This is not a novel concept, either, if you're familiar with the notorious loss of battle plans to the Germans in WWII's Operation Market Garden, to name one of history's many disastrous intelligence failures.)

One should not rule out insider attacks, either. Distasteful as it may be to contemplate, this is a very real problem. When Private Bradley Manning (later Chelsea Manning) walked out of mobile intelligence trailer in Iraq with 750,000 sensitive military and diplomatic documents copied onto portable storage media, she was demonstrating the vulnerability of data at the edge. She also demonstrated, if anyone was paying attention, just how flimsy security controls can be in remote military locations.

Mobile Edge Data Centers

We've discussed mobile data centers briefly, but the concept is worth a little more exploration. An edge data center on a truck offers potential value in a wide range of use cases. Here are a few examples:

- Agribusiness—The business of agriculture has become increasingly data-driven. With IoT sensors, farmers are now using computing power to perform tasks like the analysis of soil chemistry and plant growth. These workloads can benefit from nearby computing. Data gravity is an issue, too, with potentially large volumes of data being generated far from suitable bandwidth. Agricultural processing presents a similar use case, with factories being active during the harvest season only. In this case, a mobile data center can *follow the harvest* and move from factory to factory throughout the year.

- Energy/infrastructure—Like agribusiness, the energy and infrastructure fields experience short-term needs for intense computing and data management workloads. For instance, the process of drilling an oil well requires significant computing resources to analyze geological data in real time. Oil field maintenance and pipeline inspections are similarly compute-intensive. A mobile data center than can travel to where it's needed, and then move on, is potentially valuable.

- Events—Moments when large numbers of people gather in one spot, such as a sporting event or music festival, are suitable for the presence of a temporary edge data center. The data center can handle high volumes of device connectivity— much higher than would normally be available on the site.

- Sports teams—The business of sports is also becoming highly data-driven. In motor sports, for example, racing teams now run intensive data analytics on racing telemetry and other data streams to determine the optimal way to tune their cars, and so forth. A mobile edge data center enables racing teams to run analytics at a higher rate of performance than is possible with laptops or in the cloud.

- Corporate—Businesses may find the idea of a mobile data center interesting in certain use cases. For example, if a company leases space for a call center, it might be preferable to deploy an edge data center to the site rather than build a data center in the leased space. The lease term may be too short to justify construction of an on-site edge data center or the acquisition of property for this purpose.

In some of these scenarios, the best approach might be to deploy a portable, rather than mobile data center. For instance, a data center could be placed inside a trailer and towed to a location. Like a temporary office at a construction site, it could be left in place until it's ready to be towed to its next assignment.

CHAPTER 12

Multiedge and Edge Standards

As of now, industry analysts and executive leaders at companies with stakes in edge computing are having trouble coming up with a coherent vision of edge computing as anything other than a scattered collection of limited scope implementations. Not that there's anything wrong with that. Perhaps that's all the edge will ever be: a bunch of small data centers, each serving some distinct use case in isolation.

Is there a bigger picture? Many, including me, believe there is. Though visions vary greatly, the main idea is that there will be a universal edge computing capability. It will be conceptually similar to today's cloud. Just as it is now possible to set up an AWS account and deploy digital assets to the cloud in minutes, edge customers will be able to log onto a control panel and deploy computing and storage to the edge. They will be able to find edge data centers in locations that meet the requirements of their workloads, wherever they need them.

No One Can Do This Alone

Let's assume for the sake of argument that this vision is a valid business proposition. One could probably argue that it isn't, or that it's too early to know. But, for now, let's go with it. Let it thus be stated: There will be a universal edge that's universally accessible to customers and encompassing of every desirable edge location.

In this scenario, what is clear is that no single corporate entity or industry sector can provide such a service on its own at this time. Even if a company, or an entire industry wanted to, the cost and complexity of building an ecosystem that delivers ultra-low latency anywhere, on-demand, are beyond prohibitive. For example, the estimated investment in 5G infrastructure is expected to reach nearly a trillion dollars by 2025. That figure does not include edge computing capabilities and certainly doesn't contemplate an overall edge-on-demand-everywhere solution.

No one is writing multitrillion-dollar checks for an industry that barely exists yet. There may be a U.S.$4.1-trillion edge economy coming, if you believe research by Chetan Sharma, a leading authority on the telecommunications industry. However, most companies are wisely in the *show me first* stage of thinking about it.

Furthermore, even if capital were not a barrier, no single entity or industry sector has the full range of competencies and relationships to realize an edge strategy by itself. For instance, towercos are well situated to prevail at the edge, but they have little experience in selling what amount to data center services or virtual infrastructure.

The big data center real estate investment trusts (REITs) and colo companies are great at selling data center services, but they know little about building and managing what could be tens of thousands of edge sites. Data center REITs and colo players are making small, tentative bets on edge startups so that they won't be left out of the trend, but they are not putting major money into the category yet. Similarly, the big cloud platforms are great at selling virtual infrastructure, but they currently lack the wherewithal to deploy computing at the scale and geographic variety required by the edge.

The telcos have relationships with the towercos, as well as with potential edge computing customer. However, telcos are not known for being innovative in product development. They seem to want to build the infrastructure but let someone else develop and sell edge services. This may be why Verizon recently partnered with AWS for its Wavelength Zones edge service.

How will the edge come together, then? Assuming it does (and there's always the chance it won't...), the edge will most likely take shape as a set of interoperating, interdependent sectors. Each will own and operate a piece of the bigger system.

The best way to visualize how this might work is to think about the edge from the customer's perspective. Imagine an enterprise that needs ultra-low latency in a 100 locations spread out across the United States. These might be branch offices or warehouses, for example.

What will it take for that customer to execute this plan? Today, this means selecting sites, one at a time, buying the hardware, and arranging for consultants to make all of the locations function properly and securely. Other vendors would comprise a collection of colo providers, telcos, and/or network providers and not a few property owners.

The customer would bear the burden of procuring and paying for the equipment, locations, and services. They would then need to integrate these remote micro data center sites into their infrastructure and cloud management systems. Now, picture what would happen if this client needed 1,000 or 10,000 edge sites ....

The alternative to this messy scenario would be a situation where the enterprise could turn to one vendor, such as a telco or edge cloud provider, and say, "We need 100 edge sites in the following locations. Make it happen." The telco could then, in turn, work with whatever towerco and colo partners it needed to implement the project in all of its geographic diversity—delivering a unified service to the client, on an OpEx basis, including a single management console to monitor and manage the entire edge environment.

The Pivotal Question: Who Owns the Edge Customer Relationship?

Ultimately, the path to success at the edge will depend on who owns the customer relationship. Operationalizing the edge means converting a customer's need to be at the edge into a practical, affordable reality. Whoever has the means to accomplish this goal will own the customer relationship. The alternative is also worth contemplating: If no one has the ability to convert customer needs into a practical reality, then no one will own the customer relationship, and success in edge computing will become monstrously challenging.

A better way to ask the question might be, "How will the customer relationship be owned?" What toolsets will enable the operationalization of edge strategies? I don't have an answer, but I can take a guess. My instinct is that today's leading management platforms for on-premises infrastructure, the cloud, and networks will serve as the starting points for the true journey to the edge.

Let's go back to the earlier scenario. An enterprise wants 100 edge sites. They are more likely to go with a solution that starts with "Add them to your HPE Greenlake solution" or "Add them to your AWS console" than a solution that requires setting up an entirely separate management system and network of vendor relationships. For this to work, however, these management systems must have what I would call a *multiedge* capability. They will have to integrate with and orchestrate all the various industry players (telcos, towercos, colos, etc.) that bring the edge to life.

Making Multiedge a Reality

Multiedge is analogous to multicloud. A multiedge solution is one that enables the customer to deploy edge computing capacity to any location, on-demand, regardless of who provides it. A multiedge vendor provides this full edge service transparently to the customer. The customer does not need or want to know what technical processes are occurring to make edge computing available at any desired scale.

The difference between multiedge and multicloud is that it's a good deal more complicated to put into practice. Without downplaying the technological innovations underpinning multicloud solutions, they are tasked only with coordinating infrastructure across multiple cloud platforms. In some cases, a multicloud solution will need to integrate with on-premises IT, private cloud instances, or even satellites in orbit. A multiedge use case is significantly more complex.

A multiedge customer might need half a dozen ultra-low latency sites in New York City, 300 micro/edge data centers sitting below 5G towers in Montana, and edge data centers convenient to a few dozen offices scattered around the Midwest. Each site could have its own capacity and configuration needs, with the New York sites requiring *bare metal* servers with CPU encryption, while the Montana sites could require virtual *edge cloud* instances that only need to handle light data loads.

Working from the assumption that any introduction of manual processes or one-off negotiations with vendors will be a project-killer, the multiedge solution and vendor must make the instantiation of these sites as seamless and transparent as possible. What this will mean in actuality is hard to say, but the capabilities involved are clear enough.

MEMO and MELT

A multiedge solution, and the business that operates it, need to have a way to identify precise locations of existing edge data centers or MEC sites and/or the equipment on their racks. It needs to facilitate the subletting of this capacity from its owner on an automated basis. If a site does not exist in a desired location, the multiedge solution has to offer a streamlined mechanism for identifying a suitable site and erecting an edge/ micro data center on that spot or sending a mobile edge data center and connecting it to relevant fiber optic networks. After deployment, the multiedge provider needs to ensure security, monitoring, maintenance, and support for the sites. Figure 12.1 shows some of the capabilities required for location-centric edge management.

Integration and workflow orchestration are critical to success. The multiedge solution has to be able to connect with the core systems of

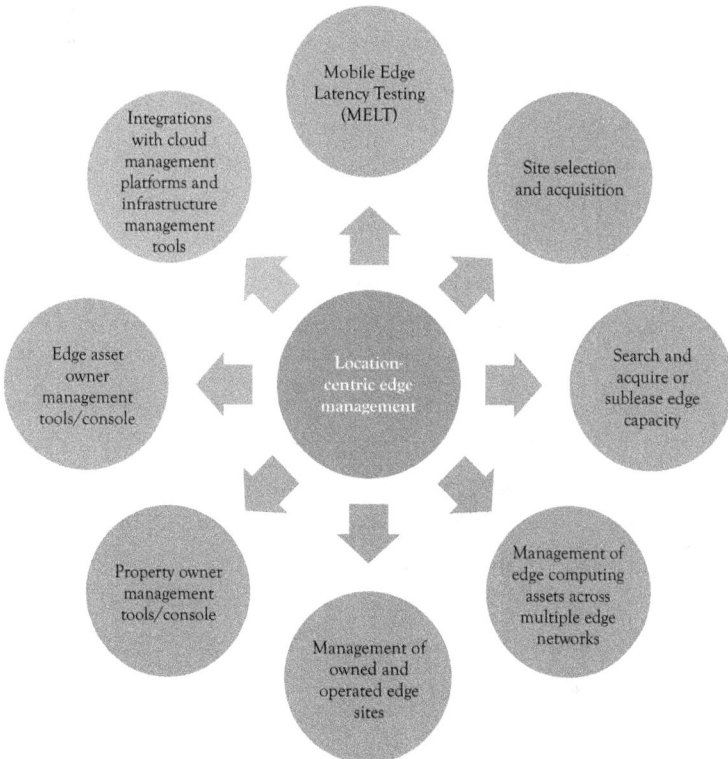

Figure 12.1 Functionality required to realize a true multiedge capability

all the sector's diverse players, for example, getting instant edge rack inventory from telcos and towercos that run edge data centers.

The realization of a multiedge capability is as much about business relationships as it is about technology features and integration. A multiedge solution has to facilitate the execution of potentially complex contractual relationships between different companies. For example, if the customer needs to rent a rack in each of a towerco's micro/edge data centers in Montana, the multiedge solution should ideally be able to handle that legal agreement.

What will this actually look like? We're getting deep into hypothetical territory here, but answering this question is the task my company, Edge Site Partners, has taken on.

Location-Centric Edge Management

A true multiedge capability needs to be location-centric. This may sound obvious, but you might be surprised to see how unaware many of today's leading infrastructure and cloud management technologies are about hardware locations. The edge, of course, is all about location, so there's a big gap to close here.

To operate at the edge, you need to know, first, where your users are, and then, whether there is edge computing capacity near enough to serve those users. If there is no capacity, you need to identify suitable sites, deploy edge data centers to those sites, and then manage them remotely. As of today, none of this is possible with any degree of efficiency.

For these reasons, we are positing a need for a new location-centric edge management platform. It will embody a concept we call MEMO, for multiedge management and operations. This is a hypothetical platform, designed in PowerPoint, the programming language allegedly favored by Oracle Chairman Larry Ellison. It's an idea, perhaps good, perhaps bad. But, in our view, it's an idea worth considering because it addresses a variety of unmet needs in what looks like a major category of IT.

A location-centric edge management platform should offer the following areas of functionality:

- Mobile edge latency testing (MELT)—A specialized testing capability is needed to determine the latency of an edge application on a location-by-location basis. With data from such a testing process, the application owner can learn where the app has sufficient edge computing capacity and where it needs more edge locations to support its SLA.

- Site selection and acquisition—An edge computing provider will need an efficient way to identify suitable locations for edge data centers—a sort of *Zillow* for edge data centers, if you will. This would mean offering detailed interactive mapping capabilities that show a prospective edge data center operator the location of available parcels of land, properties for lease, fiber optic cables, electric power, and zoning. It would also facilitate contact and deal making between the edge operator and property owners.

- Search for and sublease edge capacity—If an edge operator finds an existing edge data center in a desired location, he or she should be able to arrange subleasing of edge capacity from that data center. This would be akin to Airbnb for edge data center capacity. The location-centric platform should facilitate this process in both technical and business terms. The platform should enable the edge operator to deploy applications and data to the designed subleased data center space, either on a virtual or bare metal basis. The commercial terms of the transaction, including payment, should also flow through the platform.

- Management of edge computing assets across multiple edge networks—As the edge operator deploys instances of its software and data across data centers owned by different entities (e.g., by Verizon and AT&T), it needs a way to manage all of those instances efficiently. The location-centric platform should provide this capability.

- Management of owned and operated edge sites—If an edge operator owns multiple edge data centers, it needs a way to manage them efficiently and economically. The location-centric platform should enable rich monitoring and management capabilities for multiple owned and operated sites.

- Property owner management tools/console—The owners of properties used for edge data centers have to have a way to track their edge data center leases. The location-centric platform needs to offer this functionality. Without it, the edge operators and property owners will have to work together using manual processes. This will not scale well.

- Integrations with cloud management platforms and infrastructure management tools—It is a virtual certainty that edge operators will need to link systems running on their edge sites with systems hosted on cloud platforms, colo facilities, or in on-premises corporate data centers. It is essential that the location-centric edge management platform offers in-depth integration and interoperation capabilities with cloud management and infrastructure management platforms.

Will this come to pass? It's impossible to know. And, for sure, if multiedge becomes a real thing, it will likely look different from this set of ideas. The basic drivers of multiedge exist, however, so it's probable that some version of MEMO and MELT will come into existence.

Edge Standards: The Edge Will Have to Be a Team Effort

For pervasive micro edge computing to happen, though, a diverse group of businesses will need to find a way to work together. No one can do it alone. Multiedge offers a solution. With multiedge, the customer can realize a sophisticated edge strategy by transparently engaging with any number of supporting businesses.

Realizing multiedge will require, in my view, the development of open standards and open-source APIs. Edge Site Partners is leading an effort to create what we call Edge Location Management and Operations Standards (ELMOS). If the standards and open-source process occur, it will probably take place under the auspices of a nonprofit organization like ETSi, GSMA, or the Linux Foundation, with a *benevolent dictator* corporation supporting and guiding the effort. These will be welcome events, as they will enable multiple stakeholders, each with divergent interests, to come together for mutual gain.

Current Edge Standards Projects

The major standards bodies are engaged in developing standards for a wide range of edge computing use cases. Briefly, these include:

- Telecommunications Industry Association (TIA)—Is promulgating their standard ANSI/TIA-942-B, which describes the infrastructure requirements and design guidelines for edge data centers, including pre-processing of data, virtual RAN (V-RAN) functions deployment, and other functions enabled by proximity to the end-users.
- Groupe Speciale Mobile Association (GSMA)—Has published its Telco Edge Requirements document, *Operator Platform*, which intends to provide a common solution for operators to expose the capabilities of their networks to enterprise customers and developers allowing monetization of those capabilities.
- 3rd Generation Partnership Project (3GPP)—Has issued 3GPP SA2, which defines how user traffic is routed to the appropriate application servers in edge clouds, along with the means for applications to provision traffic steering rules.
- European Telecommunications Standards Institute (ETSi)— Has developed an extensive specification for MEC. The ETSi MEC Industry Specification Group (ISG) specifies the elements that are required to enable applications to be hosted in a multivendor multiaccess edge computing environment—as well as enabling applications and services to be hosted *on top* of mobile network elements, that is, above the telco network layer.
- Linux Foundation Edge (LFEdge)—Comprises an umbrella organization that has the goal of establishing an open, interoperable framework for edge computing independent of hardware, silicon, cloud, or operating system.

Hypothesis and Drivers of Need

The excellent work being done by these groups is establishing the basis for pervasive edge computing at the operating system, device, and software layers. Existing open standards projects and commercial platforms for edge computing do not offer much for the management of multiple edge data center locations, however. Few, if any, standards or commercial platforms are emerging to handle what could be the hundreds of thousands of physical edge data centers needed to support pervasive edge computing use cases.

Additionally, few, if any, emerging standards or commercial platforms appear able to handle edge computing deployments that span multiple edge network providers. It is a virtual certainty that edge applications will need to deploy across multiple edge networks, however. With MECs, this is known as MEC federation. Standards are evolving but have not addressed the location issues required for success.

For example, no single telecom provider can provision an application that supports assisted driving or autonomous vehicles along America's four million road miles. To work, that application would have to be deployed on multiple telecom service provider edge networks. The infrastructure to support the application could easily encompass 100,000 micro edge data centers. (Assuming 10 percent of roadways need the service, with an edge data center positioned every four miles.)

Consider the infrastructure management requirements that come with such a deployment:

- Provisioning applications and data on a location-centric basis, for example, we need to identify available edge data center rack space, each within ¼ mile of 100,000 specific locations. (And, if an existing edge data center is not present, we need to contact property owners and explore the idea of building one on their land and/or acquiring the property for that purpose.)
- Facilitating transactions to deploy across multiple edge networks, for example, we need to sublease rack space (or kWs of data center capacity) in 100,000 micro edge data centers owned and operated by five different telecom and tower providers—including requesting the sublease, procuring the capacity, negotiating a service contract(s), arranging for physical support providers on a local basis, and handling payments.
- Enabling interoperation between edge applications hosted at micro data centers owned by different corporate entities.

- Monitoring hardware and responding to outages or performance problems on a location-by-location basis, for example, a server running the EVE operating system at the micro data center at Latitude: 41.495722 | Longitude: -81.519856 is down—and repeat this use case across 100,000 sites.

- Managing infrastructure on a location-by-location basis, for example, updating the EVE operating system at a handful of locations among 100,000 sites.

- Responding to physical issues on a location-by-location basis, for example, rolling a truck to investigate vandalism at that location or summoning a utility to reconnect a power line, and so on.

- Provisioning location-sensitive failover instances, for example, we need an instance within ¼ mile of Latitude: 41.495722 | Longitude: -81.519856 in order to maintain 1 millisecond latency.

At this time, it does not appear that existing standards projects or commercial platforms either have, or are developing, such location-centric infrastructure management capabilities. Using manual methods to manage such massively distributed and multisupplier infrastructure is prohibitively expense and slow.

Proposed: ELMOS and Universal Service Edge (USE) Standards

Key edge computing stakeholders would benefit from coming together to define and develop standards for the interoperation and management of edge data center locations. The goal should be to develop standards that can handle the exchange of data required for location-centric edge infrastructure management and multiedge computing, for example:

- The location of an edge data center
- The available infrastructure elements (compute, storage) at an edge data center
- An edge data center's capacity (e.g., kilowatts, rack space, etc.)
- Commercial terms of subleasing of edge data center capacity

- An edge data center's owner and operator
- Local utility and physical support contact information for an edge data center
- Billing and commercial transaction data for procuring use of an edge data center
- Requirements needed to deploy software to an edge data center site, based on location
- Data to support monitoring and management of edge infrastructure, based on location

These standards might include automation and AI-driven orchestration of infrastructure management and commercial relationships on the basis of location. To realize these ideas, we suggest the creation of ELMOS.

ELMOS could also take the form of APIs that enable the envisioned interoperation of various components and entities involved in edge computing. These APIs might comprise a USE. Each API would be considered a USEful API, enabling location-centric infrastructure management and multiedge functionality.

Stakeholders

A partial list of industries that have a stake in location-centric edge infrastructure management and multiedge computing includes:

- Telcos—that want to offer edge computing services as part of their 5G service portfolios.
- Colocation providers—whose clients may want to add edge capabilities to existing infrastructure that's colocated in core data centers.
- Data center REITs—that also have clients with an interest in adding edge deployments to existing infrastructure hosted in their facilities.
- Public cloud platforms—that may want to add edge deployment to their portfolio of virtual infrastructure services.

- Edge cloud providers—that need to deploy edge instances in multiple locations.
- Towercos—that may want to offer edge services to their telco clients.
- Corporations—that have localized computing needs that are suitable for the edge, for example, retailers or manufacturers who deploy sensors (Industrial IoT or IIoT).
- Technology companies—that want to speed up their service offerings or deliver new services, such as metaverse experiences, for example, Facebook, Apple, and Google.
- Internet service businesses—that want to speed up or enhance their service offerings, for example, faster mobile map rendering.
- Traditional businesses with a compelling edge use case— that need edge computing to realize a business strategy, for example, car companies that want to be leaders in autonomous vehicles.
- Space businesses—that want to link terrestrial Internet users with satellites, among other use cases.
- Support service providers, spanning physical maintenance, security, IT support, and more.
- Property owners who may want to sell or lease property for use as edge data centers.
- Smart city providers and/or municipalities who want to deploy edge computing in their locations.

Hypothetical ELMOS Use Case: Making V2X and MEC Work in the Real World

The world of connected cars and vehicle-to-anything (V2X) connectivity is experiencing an exciting moment. As a growing number of 5G-enabled vehicles hit the road, standards like 3GPP are making possible a range of V2X use cases. Providing this connectivity are budding alliances between automotive companies and telecom carriers for the deployment of MEC instances at RAN sites.

So far, so good, but it's time to take a hard look at the practicalities involved in deploying V2X software at MEC sites, which will likely take the form of micro data centers set up at the bases of cell towers along the road. The following scenario lays out some of the challenges. Imagine that you're driving from Madill, Oklahoma, to Ardmore, a distance of 25 miles on Route 70.

A connected car will likely need to interact with six MEC instances along the way, approximately one every five miles. Figure 12.2 shows the actual location of the towers, based on data from the U.S. Federal Communications Commission (FCC).

These six towers are owned by five different towercos. This kind of heterogeneous tower ownership is a common phenomenon across the United States. While several large towercos own the majority of towers, over a 100 smaller towercos are part of the cell tower landscape. The tower-by-tower ownership along any given roadway will inevitably be mixed.

This ownership pattern creates a number of IT operations challenges for the owner of the V2X software. The V2X software has to be installed and managed on MECs owned and controlled by SBA, CCATT, US Cellular, Chickasaw, and SMG Ardmore.

As any experienced infrastructure manager will tell you, this is a potentially huge burden. To get the V2X software deployed and support it in production, the software owner must be able rent rack space at each MEC, which requires some kind of legal agreement and commercial transaction. They need to monitor the V2X app's performance and availability across six MECs controlled by five corporate entities. They have to support, patch, and update the app as needed on a timely basis. They need to be able to communicate with each MEC owner. And, they have to stay on top of security and respond quickly to incidents and outages. Figures 12.3 and 12.4 show the locations and ownerships of cell towers along the route.

To realize these practical objectives, the V2X software owner and MEC owner must be able interact seamlessly and efficiently. The V2X owner needs to know the MEC's exact location, the name of its owner and operator, what infrastructure elements are available at the MEC, for example, computer hardware, the tech stack, and so on, its

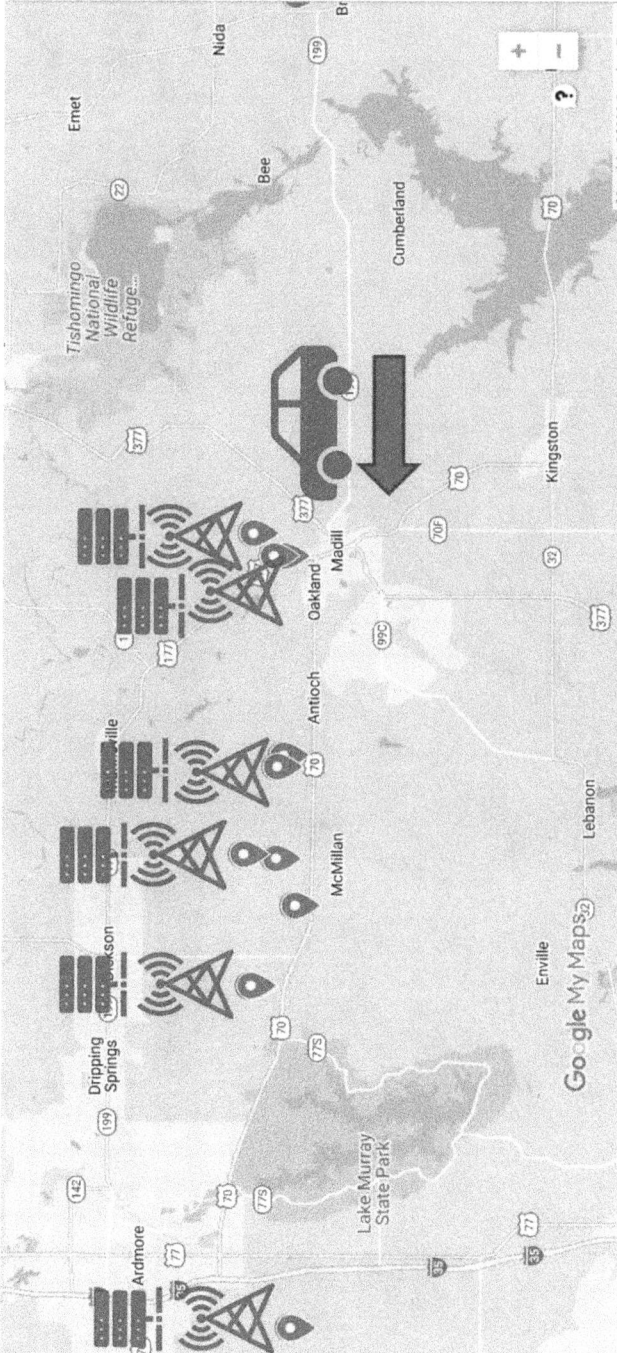

Figure 12.2 *A connected car driving from Madill, Oklahoma, to Ardmore will need to connect with six MEC sites on its 25-mile journey*

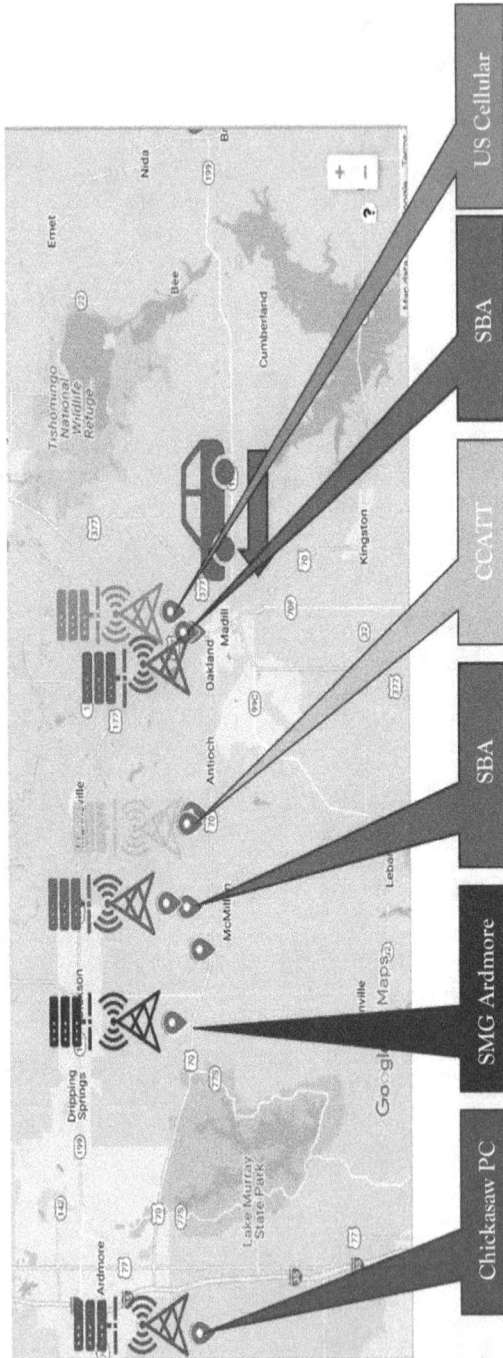

Figure 12.3 The six MEC sites on the route are owned by five different towercos

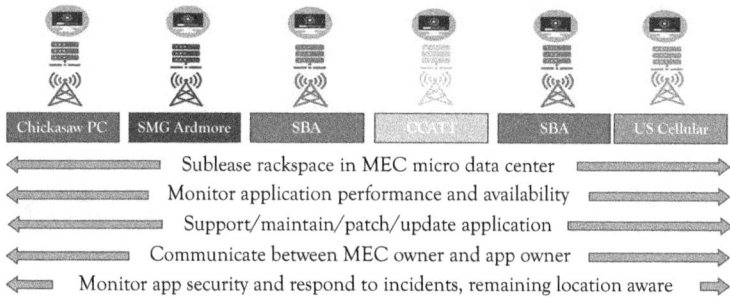

| Chickasaw PC | SMG Ardmore | SBA | CCATI | SBA | US Cellular |

Sublease rackspace in MEC micro data center

Monitor application performance and availability

Support/maintain/patch/update application

Communicate between MEC owner and app owner

Monitor app security and respond to incidents, remaining location aware

Figure 12.4 Some of the location-based tasks that a V2X use case must address across MEC sites owned by multiple towercos

capacity in kilowatts, the terms of the rack rental agreement—as well as which local service providers and utilities are supporting the V2X instance.

The V2X-MEC operational challenges can be solved, however. It won't be easy, but success will involve infrastructure management automation powered by open standards for multiedge computing like ELMOS or their equivalent. No manual solution will ever be efficient or scalable enough to work.

Conclusion

What Comes Next?

Much of this book has involved making predictions about the future of edge computing and edge data centers, so it may seem odd to devote a chapter to what comes next. I think it's worth differentiating between what's on the verge of happening versus the longer-term future. You could argue that this means going from guesswork to wild guesswork, but the thought process is worthwhile for anyone contemplating an investment in edge data centers.

The *Might Nots* of the Edge

A friend has teased me that edge data center category might develop into a *zero-billion dollar a year industry*. This is an exciting, if somewhat confusing, moment for edge data centers. The economic potential for this technology category seems huge. The technology trends driving interest in edge computing make the proliferation of edge data centers seem inevitable. Yet, just how the edge data center market segment will take shape and who will be in the lead remain to be seen.

It's possible that *the edge* will never come together as an ecosystem where customers can deploy edge data centers wherever they're needed for edge computing workloads. That is always a possibility when a new technology comes on the horizon. Will it work out the way people want it to? This book has explored a lot of what might be with the edge. A number of *might not* scenarios are deserving of attention as well.

The amount of innovation and experimentation taking place is a good sign, however. The major players in the category are all developing proofs of concept and small-scale implementations of micro edge data centers. Their strategies and prospective workloads vary, so the path to any kind of universal edge will probably not be straight or easy to follow. A *killer app* does not yet exist.

It is far from inevitable that the landscape will be dotted with thousands of micro data centers, each processing signals from nearby mobile devices. There could be some huge advance in bandwidth, for example, that enables existing antenna and data center infrastructure to handle the load at lower levels of latency than are now possible.

Alternatively, the device cluster concept could render the idea of edge data centers moot. If every smartphone functions as spare computing capacity for its neighbors, it may not be necessary to deploy edge data centers. The latency problem could also potentially be solved by rearchitecting mobile apps so that less computing needs to be done on the server side.

The hairpin problem of telecom networks could also be a showstopper. It may be too costly and complicated to reengineer phone company networks for the sake of edge computing. The cost could push the industry to find alternative solutions.

The customers may not appear, too. That's probably the biggest threat to the whole idea. Maybe there simply won't be the demand so many people are forecasting. This seems unlikely, given the proliferation of mobile devices and the increasing density of cellular antennas, but the question remains: will all this growth translate into more paying customers? It may not.

The Incredible Shrinking Edge Data Center

Looking ahead, another obvious problem that few people seem to want to discuss is the lack of space for edge data centers. In urban areas in particular, even a casual glance at fiber, power, and zoning makes it fairly obvious that there are not enough suitable sites for edge data centers. What this may cause, in practical terms, is a move to smaller form factors.

If it's impractical to deploy 100,000-pound, 1,500-square-feet modular data centers in urban areas, the solution might be to shrink the edge data center and install them in places that don't require land or commercial space. For instance, it might be more workable to deploy tiny data centers, like 6U enclosures that can fit in steel boxes mounted to telephone poles. They won't require land-use permissions and so forth. They could be paired with micro-cell antennas. The monitoring, management, and security challenges get harder with a larger number of smaller units, but this is how the space problem may get solved.

Who Is Going to Do This?

Right now, a couple of loosely connected industry segments are making small moves toward the kind of pervasive, highly localized micro edge data centers envisioned in this book. This makes a lot of sense, given that the market for such data center services is still small. Its future size is unknown, and big predictions are treated with justifiable skepticism.

With that in mind, will anyone make a bold move and get the edge business going? You could argue that some companies already have. Vapor.io, for example, has raised tens of millions in investment capital and is now deploying hundreds of edge instances. Will big companies do the same? That's less likely, given their entirely logical and wise practice of investing in proven markets versus placing big bets on speculative ideas.

What will probably happen is that each major company and industry segment that's adjacent to the edge will make incremental, reactive moves until the edge reaches a critical mass—or doesn't. The public cloud platforms might keep expanding their edge offerings, which are now based on massive edge *zones* rather than localized micro edge data centers. They could pivot and partner with owners of networks of micro data centers.

Or, the telcos and towercos could make a commitment to the edge and starting making bigger investments in edge infrastructure. This is already starting to happen, but their moves are small and tentative. It is possible that such investments by telcos and towercos could form a synergy with a push to the micro edge by the public cloud. That could just the catalyst the edge needs to become a reality.

A customer needs to present itself first for any of this to occur, however. This might be metaverses or transportation technologies, but these potentialities remain uncertain. If customers don't appear, none of this will happen. The edge will bumble along in pieces and perhaps never amount to much.

If the Edge Works, Industries Will Change Shape

I started the book by discussing the trajectories of technological revolutions. Having gone through different aspects of the edge data center and looked at relevant industry trends, it's worth taking a moment to return to theme of revolution. Specifically, what often gets missed in the analysis of current events is the potential and probability for companies and industry segments to change as a revolution gets underway.

Technological revolutions build some companies and tear apart others. In 1980, the year before it introduced the first PC, IBM was the world's largest technology company. Since then, its invention changed the technology industry so completely that IBM now makes most of its money through services. In 2004, Apple didn't make phones. Now, it's the world's leading maker of phones. Microsoft wasn't in the cloud business until it was, and now it's a dominant global player.

The edge will likely deliver similar effects on industries like telecommunications and data center real estate. Growth at the edge, should it occur as many envision, will change the structure and complexion of telecom companies, towercos, data center REITs, and others. The enterprise technology field will evolve to meet edge demands. Therefore, it would not be wise to judge the future of the edge by today's industry parameters.

Buckle Up. This Is Going to Be Exciting!

As for me, I'm optimistic about the edge. I wouldn't have started a company and written a whole book about edge computing if I were not a passionate believer in its viability as a business. Wherever I look, I see the potential for growth and opportunities at the edge. I also see challenges, to be sure. It would be crazy not to weigh the chance for success against the hard work that needs to be done to get there. I think the various industries involved are up for doing what it takes to make the edge a success.

If you are involved in edge computing, or thinking about getting started, I think you've chosen a great moment to jump in. There are deals to be done, and money to be made. I will promise you this: it won't ever be boring. I wish you great success.

Appendix

Companies and Products Referenced in This Book

- Akamai
- Amazon Web Services
- Chatsworth Products
- Compass Data Centers
- Dell
- Edgevana
- FiberLocator
- Google Cloud Platform
- Hewlett Packard Enterprise
- Inversion6
- Microsoft Azure
- NodeWeaver
- Nutanix
- RakworX
- Uptime Institute
- Vapor.io
- VMware

About the Author

Hugh Taylor, CEO of Edge Site Partners, has worked in the twin fields of cybersecurity and enterprise technology for over 20 years. As a writer, he has created content for such clients as Microsoft, IBM, SAP, HPE, Oracle, Google, and Advanced Micro Devices. He has served in executive roles at Microsoft, IBM, and several venture-backed technology startups.

Taylor has been a lecturer at the University of California, Berkeley's Law School, and Graduate School of Information. He is the author of the books *Digital Downfall: Technology, Cyberattacks and the End of the American Republic, B2B Technology Marketing, Event-Driven Architecture: How SOA Enables the Real-Time Enterprise, The Joy of SOX: Why Sarbanes-Oxley and Service-Oriented Architecture May Be the Best Thing That Ever Happened to You*, and *Understanding Enterprise SOA.*

Taylor has delivered presentations at industry conferences such as the Institute of Internal Auditors (IIA), the Microsoft SOA and Business Process Conference, the HP Technology Forum, and IBM Rational DeveloperWorks. He has consulted with dozens of entrepreneurs and crafted business plans that have helped these new ventures get funded. Taylor earned his AB, Magna Cum Laude from Harvard College in 1988 and his MBA from Harvard Business School in 1992. He lives in Cleveland, Ohio, with his wife and three children. Prior to working in the technology field, Taylor was a producer of TV movies.

Contact: hugh@edgesitepartners.com

About Edge Site Partners

Edge Site Partners, LLC (ESP) is a company committed to addressing the real estate challenges posed by the edge computing revolution. Cofounded by Hugh Taylor and Marc Feldman, ESP is developing a platform for multiedge computing, facilitating real estate transactions and financing for edge sites and putting together edge real estate deals. The company is exploring opportunities to develop and operate its own edge data centers.

www.edgesitepartners.com

Index

OTHER TITLES IN THE COLLABORATIVE INTELLIGENCE COLLECTION

Jim Spohrer and Haluk Demirkan, Editors

- *Journey to the Metaverse* by Antonio Flores-Galea
- *Doing Digital* by Ved Sen
- *Breakthrough* by Martin Fleming
- *How Organizations Can Make the Most of Online Learning* by David Guralnick
- *Teaching Higher Education to Lead* by Sam Choon-Yin
- *Business and Emerging Technologies* by George Baffour
- *How to Talk to Data Scientists* by Jeremy Elser
- *Leadership in The Digital Age* by Niklas Hageback
- *Cultural Science* by William Sims Bainbridge
- *The Future of Work* by Yassi Moghaddam, Heather Yurko, Haluk Demirkan, Nathan Tymann and Ammar Rayes
- *Advancing Talent Development* by Philip Gardner and Heather N. Maietta
- *Virtual Local Manufacturing Communities* by William Sims Bainbridge
- *T-Shaped Professionals* by Yassi Moghaddam, Haluk Demirkan and James Spohrer
- *The Interconnected Individual* by Hunter Hastings and Jeff Saperstein

Concise and Applied Business Books

The Collection listed above is one of 30 business subject collections that Business Expert Press has grown to make BEP a premiere publisher of print and digital books. Our concise and applied books are for...

- Professionals and Practitioners
- Faculty who adopt our books for courses
- Librarians who know that BEP's Digital Libraries are a unique way to offer students ebooks to download, not restricted with any digital rights management
- Executive Training Course Leaders
- Business Seminar Organizers

Business Expert Press books are for anyone who needs to dig deeper on business ideas, goals, and solutions to everyday problems. Whether one print book, one ebook, or buying a digital library of 110 ebooks, we remain the affordable and smart way to be business smart. For more information, please visit www.businessexpertpress.com, or contact sales@businessexpertpress.com.

www.ingramcontent.com/pod-product-compliance
Lightning Source LLC
Chambersburg PA
CBHW061324220326
41599CB00026B/5029